The
Frazzled Parents'
Guide to *Less Stress*

The Frazzled Parents' Guide to *Less Stress*

A **40-Day** Devotional for Releasing Anxiety and Tension When Life Feels Overwhelming

Kristin Faith Evans

WaterBrook

WaterBrook

An imprint of the Penguin Random House Christian Publishing Group, a division of Penguin Random House LLC

1745 Broadway, New York, NY 10019

waterbrookmultnomah.com

penguinrandomhouse.com

Interior illustrations: Adobe Stock: **Taiga:** watercolor border (title page, part title pages); **Alex:** additional watercolor splashes

Library of Congress Cataloging-in-Publication Data
Names: Evans, Kristin Faith, 1980- author
Title: The frazzled parents' guide to less stress / Kristin Faith Evans.
Description: First edition. | New York, NY : WaterBrook, [2026]
Identifiers: LCCN 2026010804 (print) | LCCN 2026010805 (ebook) | ISBN 9798217152032 hardcover | ISBN 9798217152049 ebook
Subjects: LCSH: Anxiety—Religious aspects—Christianity | Parenting—Religious aspects—Christianity | Peace of mind—Religious aspects—Christianity | Child rearing—Religious aspects—Christianity
Classification: LCC BV4908.5 .E927 2026 (print) | LCC BV4908.5 (ebook)
LC record available at https://lccn.loc.gov/2026010804
LC ebook record available at https://lccn.loc.gov/2026010805

Printed in the United States of America

1st Printing

First Edition

The authorized representative in the EU for product safety and compliance is Penguin Random House Ireland, Morrison Chambers, 32 Nassau Street, Dublin D02 YH68, Ireland. https://eu-contact.penguin.ie

Book Team: Editor: Leslie Calhoun • Production editor: Jessica Choi • Managing editor: Julia Wallace • Production manager: Katie Zilberman • Copy editor: Lisa Grimenstein • Proofreaders: Rachel Kirsch, Carrie Krause

Book design by Alissa Theodor

For details on special quantity discounts for bulk purchases, contact specialmarketscms@penguinrandomhouse.com.

To my fun and loving husband and two cherished children.

Thank you for teaching me to treasure every moment.

Contents

Part 3: Restoring Mind, Body, and Spirit

Part 4: Embracing Your Worth

Part 5: Drawing Closer to Jesus

Part 6: Releasing Painful Emotions

Dear Parent,

Pause for a moment. Just breathe. Just be. Inhale and receive God's peace. Exhale and release your anxieties. Breathe God's Spirit of life into your tired mind and body.

I want you to know that if you feel overwhelmed, you're not alone. About half of parents in America feel so stressed out, they have a difficult time functioning. I've been there—struggling to get through the day with very little mental or emotional energy left to focus on my husband and children.

We know all too well the problems that bombard parents from every direction. Yet most parents lack strategies to balance the intensifying pressures on their family. Our coping skills simply haven't kept up with society's accelerating pace and demands. And the idea of devoting time and energy to reading a self-help book or taking a class on stress-reduction techniques can feel unrealistic.

But excess stress can cascade into long-term health problems like high cholesterol, heart disease, chronic inflammation, hypertension, and immune disorders. We can develop mental health conditions such as depression and anxiety as well. Over time, chronic stress increases the production of hormones like cortisol and detrimentally rewires our brains. Our unmanaged stress can also negatively affect our children's development. But the healthier and more regulated we are as parents, the stronger our children will grow physically, mentally, spiritually, and emotionally.

When my daughter was young, I didn't have enough coping skills to manage the challenges of caring for her complex needs. My body's chronic stress response began to cost me my mental, spiritual, and physical health and ultimately my family's well-being. My emotional dysregulation and anxiety increased tension in our home and fostered anxiety in my children and strain on my marriage.

Determined to cultivate the skills I needed to be healthy, I sought counseling and learned new stress-reduction strategies. I also realized I desperately needed God—his strength, comfort, and power. As I discovered creative ways to connect with him throughout my day, I grew deeper in my faith. I began to thrive, and so did my family. I then went back to graduate school so I could later help other parents like you. This unique book is the product of my challenging parenting journey, two graduate degrees, years in ministry, my training and experience as a therapist, and extensive research on stress management for parents.

We often talk about stress but not the simple spiritual practices and coping tools we can use to reduce its harmful effects. Most devotional books approach stress, anxiety, and depression through faith alone, excluding the psychological aspects of faith, coping strategies, or mental health interventions. Other books focus solely on the psychological methods of reducing stress and addressing mental health disorders, in isolation from faith. But faith and mental health are interconnected and directly affect each other.

Studies have shown the powerful faith and mental health benefits of interweaving spiritual disciplines, ancient Christian traditions, and proven stress-reduction exercises. These practices combine Scripture meditation, breath prayers, and focusing on the presence of God with deep-breathing techniques, mindfulness (remaining in the present moment), and muscle relaxation.

Oftentimes we can't change our stressful circumstances, but with brief moments of mental rest and spiritual renewal, we *can* calm our central nervous systems and counteract the negative impacts of stress.

You, like most parents, may find it challenging to spend even twenty minutes reading Scripture, praying, or journaling. But those longer devotional times are important when possible. In the reality of your packed days, a more feasible approach might be taking moments throughout the day to recenter your mind on Jesus through deep breathing, reciting a Scripture verse as a breath prayer, or going for a mindful walk while focusing on God in the present moment.

I created these interactive devotionals to lead you on the journey of drawing closer to God and releasing your worries and self-defeating thoughts. I also hope to guide you in practicing skills to help you care for your mental health so you can be the best version of yourself as a parent. A healthy child begins with a healthy parent.

I will offer step-by-step guidance in developing these simple skills to help you calm your mind and body, reduce your stress levels, and lower mild anxiety and depression. By taking just a couple of minutes to use these practical tools, you can begin to positively rewire your brain, protect your mental health, and see improvements in your well-being. You will find greater joy and become a more patient and effective parent. You will begin to thrive.

Each day, I will share a short (often comical) lesson I've learned along the way and some tidbits about how that issue relates to your own stress management, spiritual growth, and mental health. Then we will walk together through

- praying a short prayer in God's presence,
- pondering a couple of questions about your life,
- practicing the simple stress-reduction exercise, and
- planning how you will apply the skill in your busy day.

The last thing I want is for you to feel pressured to quickly read through this devotional or carry guilt for skipping a day. There is no right or wrong way to work through this book. I encourage you to focus on one day and one practice at a time. Maybe even spend a couple of days on one exercise and slowly learn the skills at your own pace. My hope is that you will pause to remain in God's peaceful presence throughout your day and experience knowing Jesus in deeper and deeper ways. I pray your heart will flourish with overflowing joy and that your soul will dance in the freedom of casting off worry.

Blessings,

Kristin

A Note About Mental Health

The activities in this devotional are intended to help you grow closer to God, reduce your overall stress levels, and cope with everyday pressures in healthy ways. Applying these practices may help you improve your mood and reduce everyday worry and anxiety. But the book does not address how to treat clinical mental health disorders. Like many parents, you may be experiencing symptoms of an anxiety, depressive, or other mental health disorder. Sorting through normal reactions to parenting stress and more concerning mental health symptoms can be challenging and requires a professional mental health consultation.

A mild level of occasional anxiety or depression can be normal. But professionals typically become concerned about a person's mood or anxiety when it grows out of proportion to the situation and begins to negatively affect their daily functioning and quality of life, or if it lasts longer than two weeks. Recovering from an anxiety, depressive, or other mental health disorder often requires professional treatment and sometimes medication.

If you or others have any concerns about how your thoughts and behaviors are affecting your daily life, please seek a mental health consultation as soon as possible. If you are wishing you were dead or having thoughts about harming yourself or others, immediately call or text 988 or go to your closest emergency department. If you feel unsafe at home, please immediately seek outside help.

Part 1

Living Mindfully

DAY 1

Focus on One Moment

Come to me, all of you who are tired from carrying heavy loads, and I will give you rest.

—Matthew 11:28, GNT

As a busy mom, I usually don't take time to cook breakfast for myself, but I was craving oatmeal one morning. So I scurried around, crumbling pecans and washing fresh strawberries and blueberries. As I dashed about the kitchen, the tasks on my to-do list darted through my mind.

Email the teacher. Pick up groceries. Call the doctor.

The smell of scorching oatmeal grabbed my attention. I snatched the pot and stirred in the colorful medley. Then I realized an important ingredient was missing: cinnamon. I reached into the cabinet, grabbed the container, and generously sprinkled the finishing touch. Taking a seat at the table, I eagerly sampled a taste.

Yuck! Dropping the spoon, I cooled my stinging mouth with a gulp of water. *What is this?*

I read the spice bottle through watery eyes.

Red cayenne pepper!

And so I ate cold cereal that morning.

Do you ever feel like your mind is too full?

Parents have to become talented jugglers. We often multitask mentally, digitally, physically, and relationally. I've been that mom holding a toddler on my hip while also working on my laptop and talking with my phone clutched between my cheek and shoulder.

But multitasking is a myth. According to experts, what we are really doing is *task switching,* or leaving one project unfinished to do another. In doing so, we actually accomplish 40 percent less and are less effective, because we lose time switching mental gears (or parts of the brain). Task switching raises our stress levels, heart rate, and blood pressure and can cause burnout, anxiety, and depression. Our brains simply are not designed to multitask. It's like leaving numerous apps open on a phone to run in the background, slowing processing speed and draining the battery life.

Thankfully, practicing mindfulness can help you lower your stress levels. *Mindfulness* is simply staying in the present moment and focusing on one activity, or "single tasking." Mozart is often quoted as having given this wise advice: "The shorter way to do many things is to only do one thing at a time."

I know doing this might seem impossible, and sometimes it is. While driving your children to school, you may be practicing multiplication tables, refereeing a fight in the back seat, and inching your way through traffic. And you likely attend to your kids while you work around the house. Yet finding ways to single task, even just a few times a day, can help calm your body's stress response and improve your emotional, mental, and physical health. Single tasking will help you recharge.

When we live mindfully, giving our full attention to one activity at a time, we enjoy life more. We notice the tastes and smells of our food when we eat more slowly and savor each bite. Focusing on our conversations with others helps us build more meaningful connections. And when we wholly participate in a game, whether playing with our children or engaging in a leisure activity, we have more fun and so do others.

My taste of spicy oatmeal reminded me that God fashioned us to focus on one moment at a time. Jesus doesn't want us to carry a heavy mental load or feel stressed out. He made us to be fully engaged with others, to enjoy our days, and to give our work our best. He especially desires for us to spend time completely present with him, since he created us to know and worship him with our entire being. So focus on one moment and one task at a time and feel the weight of stress and tension lift off your shoulders.

Pray

Jesus, I feel stressed and overwhelmed. Here in this moment, I long to be fully present with you. I trust you to help me get everything done, one concern at a time.

Ponder 2 MINUTES

Take a few minutes to record your thoughts.

1. When do you find yourself task switching?

2. During those times, how do you feel inside your body?

3. What emotions come up?

Practice 3 MINUTES

Focus on the present moment.

1. Begin by taking two slow, deep breaths.

2. Sit comfortably with your feet touching the floor. Notice how the chair feels.

3. Observe your surroundings. What do you see? Smell? Hear?

4. Feel the rhythm of your breathing. Inhale. Exhale.

5. Become aware of God's presence in and around you. Rest here for a minute in the present moment.

Plan

Mindfully complete an everyday task.

1. Choose a chore to fully focus on for five minutes, like cooking, washing dishes, or doing laundry.

2. As you complete the job, use your senses:

   Notice the aromas of the ingredients and seasonings as you slowly stir the dish.

   Soak your hands in the hot, soapy water as you slowly scrub the dishes.

   Touch the texture of the clothes (and yes, even smell the dirty odors) as you place each article in the washer.

3. When your mind wanders to other needs, gently bring your attention back to your present task.

REMEMBER

Focus on one moment at a time.

DAY 2

Just Breathe

The Spirit of God has made me,
and the breath of the Almighty gives me life.

—Job 33:4

I panicked as I looked up and peered down the long pool lane. I was only halfway. I tried to regulate my breathing, but my body wouldn't cooperate. My arms and legs sank like lead, and my lungs burned. I didn't know how to swim this kind of distance.

The triathlon date raced through my mind. *I only have three months left to be able to swim a mile in open water.* I had completed shorter triathlons but signed up for this longer challenge as part of my "parenting stress-reduction plan." I was very stressed.

As I clung to the edge of the pool and struggled to catch my breath, the Olympic medalist coach knelt beside me. "I want you to hold on to the side of the pool and put your face in the water. Gently blow bubbles through your mouth for four seconds; then turn your head slightly above water and inhale for two seconds. Repeat this twenty times."

For the next six weeks, my coach instructed me in the basics of proper and efficient breathing, form, and stroke techniques. At the end of my training, I conquered that one-mile swim and crossed the finish line.

It doesn't take training for a triathlon to reduce stress levels, but it does take practicing correct deep breathing techniques. When we feel stressed, we typically breathe shallow and fast breaths and use our shoulders rather than our diaphragms. Our oxygen and carbon dioxide levels become unbalanced, making it difficult to think clearly and respond calmly. Anxiety increases, which ramps up our body's stress response system. This chain reaction can spiral without our even realizing it and make it difficult to parent calmly and effectively.

Observing our breath is the most basic form of living mindfully and is a powerful skill for reducing stress levels. Regularly practicing deep-breathing exercises can help you relax, settle your emotions, and improve your mood. The goal is to shift shallow chest breathing to abdominal or diaphragmatic breathing, which can feel opposite to how you normally breathe.

By practicing diaphragmatic breathing, or belly breathing, you can consciously control your central nervous system and relax your body and muscles. Just one five-minute session of taking slow, deep breaths can significantly lower your anxiety symptoms and physiological stress. And exhaling slightly longer than inhaling can help you relax even more. You can actually hack your mind, body, and emotions!

Ultimately, though, the designer of your body is the One who can calm your physiological, mental, spiritual, and emotional distress. God created us to take every breath in his presence and Word throughout the day. Breath prayer is an ancient Christian tradition of combining deep breathing with a short Scripture verse or prayer in harmony with God's Word. In the sixth century, St. John Climacus wrote, "Let the remembrance of Jesus be present with your every breath." Breath prayers can help us remain aware of God's presence within us as we focus on the core of our body with Christ as the center of our being. When we combine deep breathing and prayer, we experience God with our whole being—mind, body, and spirit.

While drawing us closer to God, practicing breath prayers also reduces the body's stress response, increases brain chemicals like serotonin that improve mood and lower anxiety and depression, and activates the areas of the brain that promote emotion regulation. In *Breath as Prayer,* Jennifer Tucker put it so eloquently. She wrote, "The science of breathing and the practice of praying God's Word can work hand-in-hand to help calm your body and reorient your mind toward Christ."

Perhaps God wants to take you back to the basics of simply learning how to breathe and live in him throughout your challenging day. Jesus is there in your every breath, dwelling in you and filling your whole being—your heart, mind, body, and soul. Fully inhale his breath of life and expel the toxic thoughts, emotions, and worries. Move in sync with his Spirit in this beautiful, delicate exchange, flowing between you and your Creator.

Pray

Jesus, here in this moment, I feel you breathing your life into me. Still my heart and calm my mind and body. Remind me of your presence throughout my day.

Ponder 2 MINUTES

Take a few minutes to record your thoughts.

1. Notice your breathing. How fast or slow are your breaths?

2. Where do you feel movement in your body as you inhale and exhale?

3. How calm or stressed do you feel?

Practice 5 MINUTES

Breathe with your belly.

1. Begin by taking two slow, deep breaths.

2. Place one hand on your chest and the other on your abdomen. Slowly inhale through your nose for three seconds using your diaphragm. Feel and hear the air flow in and fill your abdomen like a balloon inflating. Hold for three seconds.

3. Now gently exhale through your mouth like you're blowing bubbles. Try to exhale for four seconds. Feel the air brushing your lips as your abdomen deflates.

4. Repeat two times.

5. Now as you breathe, pray in your mind:

Inhale: *You fill me with life.*

Exhale: *I give you all of me.*

Repeat two times.

Plan

Breathe throughout the day.

Set reminders on your phone or smartwatch to prompt you to pause, become aware of God's presence, and practice this breath prayer.

REMEMBER

Breathe in God's calming presence.

DAY 3

Remain in Today

Don't worry about tomorrow, for tomorrow will bring its own worries. Today's trouble is enough for today.

—Matthew 6:34

I jolted awake. My heart was racing and I felt hot all over. My pajamas clung to me, damp with sweat. The details of the nightmare replayed in my head.

We were standing over Bethany Grace's hospital bed, waiting for her to wake up.

The surgeon sauntered in. "I wasn't able to fix her teeth. I had to pull them all." He grinned as he gave his grim report.

I felt behind me for a chair to catch me as my legs gave way. This was what I was afraid of. I knew something would go terribly wrong.

My fears had come to life in a ridiculous way.

I shut my eyes and desperately tried to go back to sleep. My daughter's dental surgery loomed in the near future. With her disabilities and airway abnormalities, she had to have routine dental work performed in a hospital operating room. I hadn't realized how much I had been worrying about the upcoming procedure and how it was affecting me. My mind and body had become so stressed I was having bad dreams and had been tossing and turning for nights.

The next day, I caught myself dwelling on the impending treatment. *What if something goes wrong? What if the surgery doesn't fix her pain?*

Then I asked myself a series of questions:

Have you done everything you can do to get her the best care possible? *Yes.*

Have you prayed about it? *Not enough.*

Is there anything else you can do about it today? *I can't think of anything.*

I took a deep breath.

Jesus, please watch over Bethany Grace and make the surgery successful.

Worrying about the future triggers our stress response (the sympathetic nervous system), raises anxiety, and activates the areas of our brains—such as the amygdala—that increase fear. When we worry, we subconsciously send our brains and bodies the message that we *should* be stressed and preparing to "fight or flight." This causes our bodies to overreact to stressors.

Yes, we face real and sometimes serious difficulties and need to problem solve and plan for our children's needs. Addressing the stressor itself can help lower our anxiety. But at the point we've done everything we can, it becomes ineffective to keep worrying. When we do, we miss out on enjoying our lives with our families or accomplishing what we can today. As Billy Graham once preached, "Some people spend so much time worrying about what might happen that they never enjoy what is happening [now] . . . Today is the tomorrow you worried about yesterday."

This is where mindfulness comes in. We live mindfully when we continually bring our awareness back to fully participating in the current moment. Remaining in the present calms those fear areas of the brain and activates the rest and relaxation nervous system (parasympathetic). We instead use the areas of our brain, like the prefrontal cortex, that help us reason, problem solve, and make decisions. We soothe our emotions and can more effectively communicate with others. But this takes intentionally redirecting our minds to the present moment throughout the day. The more we practice mindfulness, the more we become aware of when we are worrying about the future. Mindfulness is not a goal to be achieved, but rather a way of living to be cultivated.

As Christians, living mindfully centers on God's presence. Christian mindfulness is "paying attention to the present moment with Christ as the center of each moment." Christian counselors call this "Christ-centered present moment awareness." We invite Jesus and the Holy Spirit into our minds and hearts as we go about our day.

Jesus often emphasized the importance of focusing on the current day to prevent worry and anxiety. When we mentally live in the future and attempt to solve our problems on our own, we leave God out and forfeit experiencing his help and peace. God knows all that you and your family need, and he cares about you. He encourages you to continually return to him in the present moment. Pause several times throughout your day to whisper a short prayer like this: "Jesus, help me focus on today."

Pray

Jesus, draw my heart and mind back to you in this moment. Teach me how to fully live in today with you at the center.

Ponder 2 MINUTES

Take a few minutes to record your thoughts.

1. Name a specific future situation that is weighing on you right now (for example, an upcoming conference at your child's school, a meeting with your boss, or a doctor's appointment).

---

2. How is worrying about this future event affecting you today?

Practice 3 MINUTES

Come back to today.

1. Begin by taking two slow, deep breaths.
2. Think about that stressful future event for a minute.
3. Now return your focus to your breathing.
4. Sit with Jesus in this moment.
5. Prepare to begin your next task for today and give it your full attention.

Plan

Return to the present.

Each time you eat today, pause to check in with your thoughts. Bring your awareness back to sitting with Jesus and focusing on today with your family.

REMEMBER

Remain in today with Jesus at the center.

DAY 4

Accept the Present

I have learned the secret of being content in any and every situation, whether well fed or hungry, whether living in plenty or in want. I can do all this through him who gives me strength.

—Philippians 4:12–13, NIV

Thud. Thud. Thud. The sound of Bethany Grace stomping on the hardwood floor boomed throughout the house. I predicted what was coming next.

"It is time for bed." Strained patience echoed in my husband's voice. I could picture Todd's eyebrows furrowing.

I lay in bed and stared at the wall. Frustration pursed my lips. I winced as a sharp wave of pain surged down my leg. The surgery to free the compressed nerve was still a week away. I tried to distract myself from the tantrum in the other room. But the longer I struggled to ignore my constant pain and my inability to do anything about my situation, the more upset I grew. A tear formed in the corner of my eye, and I acknowledged my internal battle.

I took a deep breath and attempted to practice acceptance. *Yep, my daughter needs her mom, and my husband sure could use my help, and there's not a thing I can do about it. This is my current reality. I am choosing to trust that God is good and is here with me right now.*

Like a holiday lawn inflatable that had just been unplugged, my body relaxed, and my emotions lightened.

When we attempt to avoid our uncomfortable circumstances, we only increase our spiritual and psychological distress. Fighting reality instructs our mind and body to gear up for battle, even though we might not be able to control or change the situation. However, approaching the moment with an accepting attitude is an effective way to decompress. Practicing acceptance can reduce your body's stress hormone production and even lower your systolic blood pressure. Acceptance is fully acknowledging what your circumstances actually are without judging them as good or bad, right or wrong, or thinking it should or shouldn't be this way.

When you truly accept your present situation, you let go of struggling against reality and become willing to fully experience your current circumstances. You accept the facts with all your mind, heart, body, and soul. Acceptance is the willingness to wholeheartedly say, "Yes, this is happening, and I am feeling this way." It is *not* resigning yourself to your circumstances always being this way. It's neither approval or disapproval but rather simply agreeing that the moment is what it is. In order to change your circumstances and your life, you have to first admit the truth of what is. Maybe your child is struggling in their health, development, faith, or social interactions. To effectively help your child, you must first fully acknowledge and accept their present situation.

God is right here with us in our present reality, and our situation isn't hopeless. As Christians, we have unexplainable hope and divine help. We have faith that God can and will work in our circumstances and within us. And our joy does not depend on the current state of our lives. Sam Storms wrote, "Joy is not necessarily the absence of suffering, it is the presence of God." True joy transcends our struggles and pain. The secret to joyfully living in any and every situation is fully surrendering in the present moment and receiving Jesus's help.

To totally depend on God's strength and power, you must completely accept your present circumstances and who you are in this moment. Dallas Willard explained it this way: "God has yet to bless anyone except where they actually are . . . For those situations and moments are our life." Accepting your reality may be painful, but Jesus is right there with you in your struggles. You can make it through anything with him. I invite you to sit in this moment. Sit with your emotions. Sit with Jesus. And embrace your circumstances in his strength.

Pray

Jesus, I know you are here with me right now. With your help, I accept my present reality. I will live joyfully in your strength.

Ponder 2 MINUTES

Take a few minutes to record your thoughts.

1. What is a challenging circumstance you may be trying to avoid or reject?

2. Why do you think you might be fighting your reality?

Practice 4 MINUTES

Accept the present moment.

1. Begin by taking two slow, deep breaths.

2. Observe the facts of your current situation. Avoid judging your circumstances as good or bad.

3. Jesus is here with you. Welcome his presence.

4. Close your eyes and allow yourself to feel your emotions.

5. Open your eyes and gaze upward. Pray: "I accept my present life. Jesus, please be my strength."

Plan

Pause two times today to practice accepting your present situation.

1. State the facts and observe your emotions.
2. Say, "I accept that it is what it is right now."
3. Ask Jesus for his strength and help.

REMEMBER

Embrace your current circumstances with Jesus.

DAY 5

Parent Mindfully

Be completely humble and gentle; be patient,
bearing with one another in love.

—Ephesians 4:2, NIV

A feisty game of tug-of-war ensued. I slipped my daughter's shoe on, then she pulled it off.

"No." Bethany Grace crossed her arms and puffed her cheeks.

We stared each other down, challenging the other. No progress after fifteen minutes.

Heat rose to my cheeks. *We're going to be late to church again. What are people going to think?* I imagined us walking in during the third worship song, trying to find seats.

"Please help me put on your shoes." Impatience surged from my hands up through my shoulders to my jaw.

Why is this such a battle? If she would just cooperate. I should have gotten up earlier.

She dug in her heels. My mounting exasperation magnified her stubbornness.

Then I stopped and tried something different. Taking a slow, deep breath, I mentally stepped back and surveyed my thoughts, emotions, and tense body. I realized my mind had been in the future concocting scenarios and self-critical messages that were stirring up anxiety. I hadn't been focused on my daughter. I whispered, "Jesus, please help me love Bethany Grace well."

Curiosity prodded me. *What's going on? Is she not feeling well? Just not wanting to go to church?* I sat there simply admiring my daughter. Compassion welled up as I tried to understand her perspective. I glanced at the shoe we had been fighting over and picked it up. Something rattled inside. I reached in and pulled out a metal hair clip. I looked in my daughter's eyes, and we connected for the first time that morning. She has always been mostly nonverbal and was unable to tell me that the shoe hurt her foot. If I had been paying attention to her facial expressions, I would have noticed her pain. Not my finest parenting moment, but I did learn a valuable lesson that morning.

As parents, we can sometimes operate in a mindless mode. We mentally check out, multitask, or dwell on the past or future. But it's when we mindfully parent that we are most effective.

Mindful parenting is basically being fully mentally present in your environment and engaged with your child. To help us remember this kind of parenting, I created the acronym SLOWER.

Scan your emotions, thoughts, body sensations, impulses, and behaviors

Listen to your child with your complete attention

Observe your child's emotions, reactions, and facial expressions

Withhold judgment about yourself and your child

Extend compassion and acceptance toward yourself and your child

Respond calmly and with kindness

Mindful parents tend to be more relaxed and better able to connect emotionally with their children. When we remain in the present moment, we can parent more consistently, because we witness the factors leading up to the stressful situation. We can make well-thought-out decisions and nurture a peaceful atmosphere.

Our children mirror our emotions. When we experience stress, our tension can cause our children to feel emotionally out of sorts, which can lead to challenging behaviors. Parenting mindfully can help us reduce our reactivity by cultivating self-awareness of our own issues and emotions. When we become calmer, our children's anxiety and resistance lessen, which reduces our own stress levels. Parenting mindfully not only improves our own well-being, but it helps us grow healthier kids as well—spiritually, mentally, emotionally, and even physically. We also experience special moments with our children or opportunities to make positive memories together.

An easy way to remember to pause and take some deep breaths throughout the day is to create some "bells of mindfulness" for yourself. These are everyday situations that prompt you to practice mindfulness. Your child's laughter and cry can be simple cues. When your child laughs, it's time to breathe and enjoy the moment. When your child cries, it's time to pause and take some deep breaths.

Mindful parenting does not replace other parenting principles or take away your authority. It is simply being fully present, self-aware, and able to respond to your child's unique needs and behaviors most effectively. Refocusing your heart and mind on Jesus in your current situation will help you draw from *his* love and wisdom for your child. Awareness of his presence will guide you to parent in a more humble, patient, and compassionate way.

Pray

Holy Spirit, remind me of your presence in my parenting moments. Help me love my child with your gentleness and patience.

Ponder 2 MINUTES

Take a few minutes to record your thoughts.

1. What is a common parenting situation that tends to cause you stress?

2. How do you typically react?

3. How would you like to respond?

Practice 4 MINUTES

Rehearse your response.

1. Begin by taking two slow, deep breaths.
2. Imagine yourself in that stressful parenting moment. Observe your child and your surroundings.
3. Notice how you feel inside your body. What thoughts and emotions come up about yourself and your child?
4. How might your child be feeling?
5. Pray: "Jesus, help me sense your presence and guide me in parenting well."
6. Imagine calmly responding to your child.

Plan

Choose an opportunity today to practice mindful parenting.

You can use the above practice and the SLOWER parenting principles as a guide.

REMEMBER

Be fully present with your child in the current moment.

Part 2

Relaxing Stress Levels

DAY 6

Leave Your Worries

Leave all your worries with him, because he cares for you.

—1 Peter 5:7, GNT

I sat at the kitchen table lost in a maze of jumbled thoughts.

How are we going to get the kids everywhere they need to go? What if I forget to give Bethany Grace one of her medicines?

Cold rain tapped on the window.

How are we going to pay these bills? What should I do if her oxygen level drops?

The shower poured harder outside, drowning out my thoughts. Chilly numbness ran throughout my body and mind.

The crushing stress and my habit of worrying had fueled a severe anxiety disorder. Granted, I did have a lot of real problems to be concerned about, but my worry had grown in power and was suffocating me. The pressure had mounted to the point I couldn't function well or be effective. Anxiety was making me physically ill.

I had to do something.

I grabbed a notebook and began to list all my worries. Then I prayed about them. The dark cloud lifted some. I still had troubles, but I had more hope and was able to think clearer that day.

If you've experienced anxiety from the stress of parenting, you're not alone. The emotional weight, mental strain, and competing responsibilities can feel overwhelming at times. We can wear ourselves out by worrying and trying to provide for every single one of our children's and family's needs.

Worrying about everyday problems now and then is normal. Everyone experiences anxious thoughts from time to time. Mild levels of anxiety can help us pay attention, plan ahead, and problem solve.

But excessive worrying can create added stress. And there's a difference between worry and anxiety disorders. Worry involves temporary thoughts about specific situations, whereas anxiety is more intense, persistent, and vague and manifests in both psychological and physical symptoms. Anxiety can cause excessive and unrealistic worry as well as difficulties with concentration and problem-solving. Physical discomforts can include sweating, stomach problems, increased heart rate, hyperventilating, or feeling weak and lightheaded.

If you're experiencing moderate to severe symptoms of anxiety, you are among the 20 percent of mothers and 15 percent of fathers who report living with clinical anxiety. Parents of children with any type of disability are at even greater risk, with one in three living with a clinical anxiety disorder. I learned that recovering from an anxiety disorder typically requires professional mental health treatment, new coping skills, and sometimes medication. One strategy I now use is becoming mindful of my anxious thoughts. I name the specific worry, notice my emotional and physical reactions, and then problem solve. This practice helps reduce my stress and the tension in my body.

We can also experience anxiety on a spiritual level, a disquiet in our spirits. Sometimes we don't even realize how much we carry in our hearts until we start to surrender our burdens to God. Jesus doesn't expect us to solve our problems on our own. Pastor and author Craig Groeschel preached, "Anxiety is a signal alerting you that it's time to pray. . . . If it's big enough to worry about, it's big enough to pray about. If it's on your mind, it's on God's heart."

Consider centering your mind on Jesus for five to ten minutes. What's the worst that could happen if you don't worry for ten minutes? To bring your anxieties to Jesus, you have to first go to him. He wants you to come and give him those cares that weigh lightest and heaviest on your heart in exchange for his help, freedom, and peace. Leave your worries with him.

Pray

Jesus, I bring my worries to you, because I know you care about me. Thank you for taking my anxieties and giving me your peace.

Ponder 4 MINUTES

Take a few minutes to record your thoughts.

1. Here are some worries common to parents. Check any that resonate with you and list your own specific worries whether big or small.

Concerns about your child's well-being:

- ☐ Physical health
- ☐ Developmental milestones
- ☐ Emotional and mental health
- ☐ Education
- ☐ Social media use
- ☐ Behaviors
- ☐ Peer interactions
- ☐ Relationship with God
- ☐ Other

Additional stressors in your life:

- ☐ Balancing your different roles and your family's needs
- ☐ Finances
- ☐ Your physical health
- ☐ Your mental health

- ☐ Church or faith struggles
- ☐ Relationships with family, significant other, or friends
- ☐ Other

2. When you worry, how do you feel inside your body?

3. How might talking to Jesus about your worries help ease your angst?

Practice 4 MINUTES

Leave your worries with God.

What you will need: a pen; note cards, sticky notes, or a piece of paper torn into ten pieces; a bowl

1. Begin by taking two slow, deep breaths.
2. Use your list of worries from the Ponder section and write each one on a separate note card.
3. Hold up one worry at a time and offer it to God. Then place it in the bowl.
4. After you place the last card, hold up the bowl and pray, "I give you all my worries and anxieties, Lord."
5. Exhale. Receive God's peace.

Plan

Create a daily reminder to help you leave your worries with God.

Here are some ideas:

Post a note on your bathroom mirror or car dashboard.

Set an alarm on your phone.

Keep a stack of sticky notes on your kitchen counter to write down your worries and give them to God.

REMEMBER

Leave all your worries and cares with Jesus.

DAY 7

Surrender Control

Trust in the LORD with all your heart;
do not depend on your own understanding.
Seek his will in all you do,
and he will show you which path to take.
—Proverbs 3:5–6

Todd and I sat staring at each other. Our silent agreement draped our hearts in sorrow.

His words filled the heavy air. "All our dreams we shared on our wedding day have vanished. We can no longer serve in ministry together or go on mission trips as a family."

"And I can never get pregnant again. We'll never have a normal family life." I looked down.

Despite our determined efforts to make our dreams a reality, it had become clear that our plan was not God's plan for our family. My life was spinning out of control. I was clinging to my crumbling marriage, my spiraling mental health, our shrinking finances, and our medically fragile daughter, just trying to keep her out of the hospital. The more frantic I grew, the tighter I gripped any little thing I could control. Just when I needed to trust God more than ever, I was trying to rip control back from him.

As my anxiety and depression consumed me, I became desperate. I threw up my hands and cried out to God to ask him for help.

Todd and I began to pray, asking God to guide us. And he did.

Over the next year, he cleared a path in a big way. Due to the loss of three close family members, a house dropped in our laps four hours closer to the children's hospital and across the street from excellent schools. New career opportunities opened up for both Todd and me. God began to heal and bless our family in amazing ways.

We can influence the outcomes of many aspects of our lives. When we're successful, our stress and anxiety often lower. But so many circumstances are beyond our control. We sometimes carry the illusion that we can change people and situations, and we worry about the future. But attempting to control what we cannot control can increase stress, anxiety, and self-criticism, as well as lower our life satisfaction and the quality of our relationships.

Some areas of life allow us to effect change to a degree, but the outcomes still may be out of our hands. These include:

- job security or career path
- health and safety of our family

- behaviors of others: spouse, family members, friends, boss, co-workers
- choices our child makes
- financial stability
- decisions from professionals and agencies

Our anxiety can stem from realizing we don't know the future and don't have the power to control everything. But our peace can also come from acknowledging we don't know and don't have the power to control everything. What we *can* control is giving God control and radically surrendering to him. Don't we want the One who is all-knowing and all-powerful and who sees the big picture to be in control and lead? God's will for your life is likely different from your own plans. What society says is important and what others strive for may not be God's plan for you and your family.

But it's the not knowing and the not understanding that we can get hung up on. Increasing our tolerance of uncertainty and relinquishing control requires trusting God's goodness from deep within our heart. As Lysa TerKeurst explained, "We can't stop or control things that roll our way any more than we can stop the water's edge. But we can make the minute-by-minute choice to let our souls rest in God. . . . We don't have to understand; we just have to trust."

We can make our plans, but ultimately God is in control. He knows what will be in your very next moment and then the next. And his plans for you and your child are good (see Jeremiah 29:11). Seek his will wherever you are and in whatever you're doing, and he will smooth out the road before you in his perfect plan and will for your life (see Romans 12:2). But you have to unclench your fists and surrender control. The wider you open your hands, the more God can fill them. Hold up your hands and release your worries and fears, and then receive God's peace, blessings, and joy in exchange. Jesus stands in front of you, placing his hands on yours. You can trust him.

Pray

Jesus, you are Lord. I trust you wholeheartedly, and I give up control to follow your plan for my family and for my life.

Ponder 3 MINUTES

Take a few minutes to record your thoughts.

1. Think about a stressful situation you're attempting to control. Maybe it's an issue at work, in your marriage, or with your child.

2. How are you trying to control the situation?

3. What are your thoughts about it? Emotions? Fears?

Practice 3 MINUTES

Surrender the situation.

1. Begin by taking two slow, deep breaths.

2. Name the situation you're worried about and trying to control.

3. Tightly clench your fists and inhale through your nose for four seconds.

4. Slowly exhale through your mouth while relaxing your hands, palms facing up.

5. Pray: "God, I surrender my attempts to control ________________. I release the situation to you."

Repeat steps 2 through 5 two times.

Plan

Relinquish control two more times today.

When a stressful situation or thought comes up, practice the surrender exercise.

REMEMBER

Radically surrender control to God.

DAY 8

Calm Your Body

I have certainly soothed and quieted my soul;
Like a weaned child resting against his mother,
My soul within me is like a weaned child.

—Psalm 131:2, NASB

"Curl your toes like you're squishing mud between them. Squish. S-q-u-i-s-h. Now pull them out of the mud and wiggle them."

The lady's voice on the app sounded fun and comforting. As my kids and I followed her instructions, dimples began to appear on their flushed faces.

"Pull in your belly muscles and hold tight. A baby cow is walking over to stand on your stomach. S-q-u-e-e-z-e. Okay, she's gone. You can drop your belly."

She guided us in tensing and releasing each muscle group in our bodies, from our feet to the top of our heads. We ended by slowly exhaling like we were blowing bubbles. Our moods leveled out, and we enjoyed a pleasant afternoon. I felt grateful I had discovered this tool.

I played this meditation recording to help the kids settle down. But it reminded me of how developing the skill of calming my central nervous system in this way had helped me tremendously. I had practiced progressive muscle relaxation (PMR) exercises for years, both in my own therapy sessions and in guiding clients in learning how to cope with stress. Extensive research has shown that engaging in PMR exercises reduces stress, anxiety, and depression. Listening to a PMR meditation can also help you relax, fall asleep faster, and enjoy a higher quality of sleep. By using this skill, we also model to our children how to regulate their emotions and lower anxiety.

Guided PMR exercises lead you in tensing then releasing one muscle group at a time to help you become aware of your body sensations and recognize the difference between tense and relaxed muscles. This practice tells your brain and body, "The threat is gone. You can relax." By being fully present in your body, your focus can come back to the current moment, which reduces your anxiety. People often practice PMR for five minutes or up to thirty minutes or longer.

We tend to carry stress in our stomachs, backs, shoulders, necks, jaws, and heads, which can cause chronic headaches, stomach problems, muscle tension, stiffness, and pain. We often think of our bodies, minds, and spirits separately. But when we address our body and mind together, we discover where we carry stress and painful emotions in our body.

Like an infant learning how to self-soothe while being held by a nurturing parent, we sometimes have to relearn how to soothe ourselves in the arms of our loving God. As we grow in trusting his goodness and his care for us, we experience his peaceful embrace in deeper ways. Experts in Christian mindfulness Dr. Regina Chow Trammel and Dr. John Trent wrote, "Progressive muscle relaxation infused with God's presence sanctions our bodies to experience his soothing, holy touch." While holding us with his healing hands, he soothes not only our minds and bodies; he also heals our souls. The Hebrew root word translated as *soul* in Psalm 131:2 means "whole being," or our connected inner spirit and physical body. We experience complete wholeness and contentment in God when we invite his presence into our lives. Allow Jesus to be with you and calm your body, thoughts, and emotions so he can heal your spirit as well.

Pray

Jesus, thank you for giving me ways to relax my mind and body. Help me soothe my muscles, calm my emotions, and still my thoughts. I release all my stress to you.

Ponder 2 MINUTES

Take a few minutes to record your thoughts.

1. When you're stressed, where do you feel tension in your body?

2. What might your body be trying to tell you?

Practice 5–10 MINUTES

Simply be in your body, aware of God's healing presence.

For this exercise, you can sit comfortably in your chair with your feet resting on the floor or lie down on the floor or on your bed.*

1. Begin by taking two slow, deep breaths.

2. Continue taking deep breaths. Slowly inhale through your nose, filling your abdomen. Exhale through pursed lips, relaxing your body.

3. Imagine God's warm, peaceful light shining on your head and moving down through your body. Pray, "Jesus, please touch and calm my mind, heart, body, and spirit."

4. Beginning with your forehead, cheeks, and jaw, tense each muscle group in your body (without pain or discomfort) for about five seconds, then relax your muscles.

5. Slowly inhale as you tense your muscles. As you exhale, release your muscles and stress to God. For example, as you pull your shoulders up to your chin and then lower

* If at any time this exercise causes you discomfort or pain, stop immediately and consult a medical professional.

them, you can pray, "God, please lift this weight off my shoulders."

6. Notice your body sensations, thoughts, and emotions. Do you feel any comfort, aches, pains, looseness, soreness, tightness, or flexibility? Consider the difference between the tight muscles and the relaxed muscles. Listen to your body and emotions. Be curious about what your body might be trying to tell you.

7. You can ask God to touch and heal specific parts of your body or any painful emotions that arise.

8. After finishing with your feet, end with this prayer: "Thank you, God, for my body and for your peaceful presence in my heart."

Plan

Practice this progressive muscle relaxation exercise at bedtime this evening.

REMEMBER

Ask Jesus to help you calm your mind, body, and spirit.

DAY 9

Say No to Yes

[Jesus replied,] " 'You must love the LORD your God with all your heart, all your soul, all your mind, and all your strength [and . . .] love your neighbor as yourself.' "

—Mark 12:30–31

"Can you lead the party games? No one's signed up." The parent volunteer sounded bothered.

"Sure. I'd be happy to," I agreed without hesitating.

"Great. The party's on Thursday." Her voice switched to cheer.

Why did I just commit to that? When am I going to get this done? Am I even free that day?

I wanted to spend time in Bethany Grace's classroom and meet other parents. I also wanted this mom to like me, and I would have felt guilty not helping. I rearranged my schedule, spent time scrolling through fall party game ideas, and gathered supplies. As a result, some of my other commitments and time with family received less of my attention, and I felt even more stressed than before.

In the past I was a people pleaser. I tried to do it all, and I walked around constantly stressed and burned out. But parents can't do it all and do everything well. People who overcommit have higher levels of clinical anxiety and depression, sleep disturbances, and mental fatigue. There are three main emotional reasons we overextend ourselves: desire for validation, fear of rejection and failure, and comparison with others. We take on more to appease others, connect socially, and feel good about ourselves. When we say yes and receive approval, our brains reward us by releasing dopamine, a neurological chemical that makes us feel pleasure. And the more we say yes, the stronger this brain pathway grows.

To lower our stress levels, we need to balance how we spend our time and energy. We must give ourselves permission to say no. This may mean saying no to your child's wish to add an activity to the calendar, to a social invitation, or even to your boss pressuring you to take on a new project. More noes will equal less stress and more room for important yeses that will improve your health and your family's well-being.

One way to make it easier to say no is to allow some time away from the person making the request before you give an answer. One response I've learned to say is, "Let me get back to you soon." Using this simple phrase has been so freeing! Sometimes I agree to commit, but usually I politely answer, "I'm not able to commit to that at this time." I've discovered that sometimes the asker actually respects me more for being thoughtful and setting boundaries.

But how do we know when to say yes and when to say no? Jesus gives us an easy guide. In everything we do, we can ask ourselves, "Will this help me love God and others better?" The answer will guide us in building our priorities around Jesus's two greatest commandments. Before we make a new commitment, we must first identify and schedule our priorities ahead of time. Establishing a concrete list of your own and your family's highest values is the first step to reducing your household's stress levels. In *The 7 Habits of Highly Effective People,* Stephen Covey taught, "The key is not to prioritize what's on your schedule, but to schedule your priorities."

You can also consider these questions when deciding whether to take on an additional commitment:

- Does it align with my family's and my own priorities?
- Have I already scheduled my priorities?
- Do I have room in my schedule for this added responsibility?

We can't love God and others well if we try to do too much. We don't have endless mental, emotional, spiritual, and physical energy. Guard your time and build boundaries around your priorities. Pause before making commitments and live more intentionally. Jesus doesn't ask you to overload yourself and burn out. He simply wants you to wholeheartedly love him with every breath and generously love others.

Pray

Jesus, I love you with all my being. Teach me to spend my time and energy loving you and others more.

Ponder 2 MINUTES

Take a few minutes to record your thoughts.

1. What is something you said yes to that you've regretted?

---

2. Why do you think you agreed to it?

---

3. What is something you can currently say no to?

Practice 7 MINUTES

Identify your priorities.

What you will need: paper and a pen

1. Begin by taking two slow, deep breaths.
2. Label the first sheet of paper "Important to me." List all the aspects of your life and family that are most important to you.
3. Label the second sheet "Priorities" and underneath write, "Love God and love others." Make three columns:

"Most important," "Second most important," and "Least important."

4. Pray about your "Important to me" list, asking God which tasks and activities should take priority. Begin placing your priorities in each column.

5. Moving forward, fill your schedule first with priorities in the "Most important" column.

Plan

Prioritize your yeses.

The next time someone asks you to commit your time and energy:

1. Say you will get back to them soon.
2. Refer to your priority list.
3. Check how full your schedule already is.
4. Pray, "Jesus, should I commit to this?" and listen for his reply.
5. Respond to the person.

REMEMBER

Pause before saying yes.

DAY 10

Be Flexible

We can make our plans,
but the LORD determines our steps.
—Proverbs 16:9

I hopped into the car and turned on my favorite radio station. Then I headed for my first destination. I had my day planned out, and I was looking forward to the time to myself. After checking off my list of errands, I was going to treat myself to lunch out while I worked on my laptop.

I was happily singing while stopped at a red light when my music was interrupted by an incoming call. I looked at the car dash screen. "Middle School Nurse."

My heart quickened. *This can't be good. What's going on?*

"Mrs. Evans? Bethany Grace is okay. But she's running a fever. Can you please come pick her up?"

"Of course. I'm heading that way now. Thank you."

I clicked End. Ugh. There went my day.

Just like that, my mood dropped, and my stress level shot up. I made a U-turn and drove to the school. The remainder of the day, I grumbled and dwelled on my disrupted plans. Because I remained mentally and emotionally stuck, I missed the opportunity to focus on my extra time with my daughter and to care for her in the most loving way.

I know for me, the more stressed I am, the more I feel I need to control my schedule. So days like that used to really frustrate me. All the other days, I worried I would get a call and have to drop everything, which kept me from being mindful and enjoying the moment. Then I learned to greet each day with the expectation that my schedule might get interrupted. Now when I actually get to carry out my day as planned, I'm even more thankful. I also intentionally schedule fewer tasks to allow extra time for when those inevitable issues do come up. I anticipate traffic and extra needs my children may have.

When our expectations for the day or interactions with others don't go as planned, how we respond helps determine our moods and then our children's moods. Developing mental flexibility improves our ability to cope with stress and effectively respond to unexpected situations. Psychological flexibility involves being more open, aware, and accepting of our thoughts, emotions, and experiences in the present moment. Becoming more flexible helps improve our health and enjoyment of life. Other benefits include stronger relationships, lowered anxiety and depression, more effective problem-solving, and greater life balance. When our children need our attention, we're able to respond to interruptions more attentively and lovingly.

When an object is flexible, it more easily bends and doesn't break. Picture a willow tree with its pliable branches swaying in the breeze. Trees with more rigid branches can crack when stronger winds blow. Cultivating a flexible attitude before life's stressors hit prepares us to successfully handle our problems instead of being broken by them.

Approaching our day with a flexible mindset also encourages us to be open to listening for God's voice to direct our time, energy, words, and actions. I often pray that God will open my eyes and heart to see unexpected and unwelcomed interruptions as chances to accomplish his will. In *Everyday Joys,* Tama Fortner gracefully shared how she approaches changes in her day's plans by viewing them "not as annoyances, but as opportunities to show love and kindness, to share truth, and to point others back to the Father."

We can make our plans with our limited knowledge, but God knows how events will actually unfold and where the day will take us. He sees the stressful situations and changes to which we will need to adjust. He designed the full picture and knows how the moments we interact with others can change lives and the world. Jesus desires for you to include him in your planning process and to call on him at different points throughout the day. He asks you to be open to following his will, and moving with the guidance of his Spirit. So welcome the day with a flexible mindset and listen for Jesus's voice to guide you along the way.

Pray

Jesus, show me what my day holds and how to best spend my time in ways important to you. Help me respond to stressful situations with flexibility, creativity, and your compassion.

Ponder 2 MINUTES

Take a few minutes to record your thoughts.

1. What is a situation in which you become frustrated when you are interrupted?

2. How do you typically respond?

3. What would it look like if you approached that moment with a more flexible mindset?

Practice 5 MINUTES

Create a flexible response.

1. Begin by taking two slow, deep breaths.

2. Imagine you're in that situation and have just been interrupted. Observe all that is happening inside and around you.

3. Brainstorm different ways you could respond to this disruption with a flexible and accepting mindset.

4. Consider how Jesus might desire for you to approach the situation.

5. Describe how you feel and how you now see your day after exploring this new mindset. Imagine you're there in that situation responding in this way.

Plan

Respond to disruptions with a flexible attitude.

When you experience an interruption today, pause and respond in your new and creative way.

REMEMBER

Welcome the unexpected plan Jesus has for your day.

Part 3

Restoring Mind, Body, and Spirit

DAY 11

Retreat to the Quiet

He would withdraw to deserted places and pray.

—Luke 5:16, NRSV

The arcade tune and the whirling sound of the sit-and-spin ride grated on my nerves. A color-changing ball and flashing TV screen blazed at me as I checked on the kids squealing in the family room. Toys strewn about the space added clutter to my thoughts.

I plopped down on the couch to rest, and Bethany Grace came over and hugged me with her vanilla-scented doll. The aroma of roasting chicken and the chime of the oven timer beckoned my attention. The house felt stuffy. I realized I was still wearing my sweaty exercise clothes.

I needed a break. My brain was about to explode.

Ding. A new text message.

I wanted to cover my ears and flee the chaos. And then, that's exactly what I did.

"Let's go play outside," I suggested.

The kids jumped up, grabbed a ball, and ran to the door. I turned off the oven, and we retreated to the fresh air. While they expended energy running around the yard, I relaxed on the porch. As I escaped all the ruckus inside the house, my tension began to fade.

Have you ever felt overloaded?

As parents, we're constantly bombarded with information and sensory stimuli from emails, images on screens, ads, our kids' music, videos, and toys. Not to mention the sounds of whining, screaming, and crying, along with background noise from appliances, conversations, lights, and phone notifications. Our brains and bodies can become overstimulated and have difficulty effectively processing sensory input. It can get to the point that we try to block out certain sights and sounds, which then results in our no longer being able to enjoy the pleasant sensory experiences. We can become sensitive to touch and smells and begin to overeat and develop vision problems. Physical affection from our spouses or kids may even feel like too much.

Sensory overload causes stress on the nervous system, resulting in anxiety, irritability, racing thoughts, fatigue, difficulty concentrating, sleep disturbances, and even physical discomfort. In order to induce our body's relaxation response in stressful situations, we have to reduce sensory input and bodily movements. Studies have shown that isolating from sensory input for even brief periods at a time can decrease stress, pain, anxiety, and depression, as well as significantly improve sleep quality and optimism.

After that overwhelming day, I began to take sensory breaks and go sit on the porch. But I would often find myself using those breaks to pick up my phone and scroll through emails and social media. Then I learned the joy of putting down my phone, taking some deep breaths, and simply being in the moment. I noticed the birds' sweet melodies, the fragrance of flowers blooming, and the rustle of leaves. I began to pray and listen for the gentle voice of Jesus and wait for the peaceful breeze of his Spirit to soothe my frazzled body and mind. I relearned how to enjoy life with my senses.

I'm thankful that, over time, I've formed the habit of limiting as much sensory input as possible throughout my day. I often do things like shut my laptop, turn off bright lights, and drive in silence instead of listening to music or talking. In *Rhythms of Renewal,* Rebekah Lyons wrote, "When we carve out space for the quiet, to retreat to a silent place to pray, journal, or read, we rest from the noisy distractions of our lives. This rest pulls us out of the anxiety and stress of the world, if only for a moment."

Jesus often went away to desolate places in the desert, the wilderness, or on a mountain to escape the commotion and demands of the crowds. He was likely physically drained from people touching him, mentally exhausted from teaching and answering questions, emotionally tired from seeing the suffering of others and having intense conversations, and spiritually weary from healing others. But he was intentional in his habit of retreating to silent and remote places. He stole away to focus on communing with his Father so he could seek his guidance, renewal, and power.

In the same way that Jesus experienced weariness firsthand, he knows you're worn out and in need of a break. He is waiting for you in the stillness. Retreat with him to the quiet.

Pray

Jesus, teach me to turn off the noise so I can hear you. Help me develop the habit of withdrawing to the quiet to rest and listen to you.

Ponder 2 MINUTES

Take a few minutes to record your thoughts.

1. Reflect on all the sensory input that bombards you throughout your day (both unpleasant and pleasant). List as many noises, smells, physical touches, screens, lights, flavors, and textures of foods, beverages, and medicines you can think of.

---

2. Name at least one sensory source you can limit or eliminate.

Practice 3 MINUTES

Sit and observe with your senses.

1. Begin by taking two slow, deep breaths.
2. Close your eyes and listen for sounds.
3. Inhale and notice any smells.
4. What sensations do you feel on your body and skin?
5. Open your eyes and look around. What do you see? Observe all the sources of light.
6. Turn off or remove any unnecessary sensory inputs.
7. Sit in God's presence, listening to his Spirit.

Plan

Take a sensory break.

1. Choose a time today to take a sensory break for five to ten minutes.
2. Put away technology and turn off as many sounds and lights as possible.
3. Set a timer and spend those minutes enjoying the quiet and communing with God in silent prayer.

REMEMBER

Retreat to the quiet with Jesus.

DAY 12

Stop to Rest

It is in vain that you rise up early
and go late to rest,
eating the bread of anxious toil;
for he gives sleep to his beloved.
—Psalm 127:2, NRSVA

"Kristin, come over right now." My friend's serious tone convinced me to listen.

After going nonstop for days with little sleep, I had reached the point of exhaustion. I finished my errand and headed toward my friend's house. She walked out to meet me as I pulled into her driveway. After squeezing me tight, she led me into the house. "Would you like some water, tea, coffee?"

"Water sounds great. I'm so thirsty." I sat at the kitchen table, weary in every way.

She took a seat across from me, and we talked for a couple of minutes while I finished my water. Concern overshadowed her smile.

"You need to rest." She held out her hand and guided me upstairs.

She then prepared her bed for me. "Lie down and sleep. Rest as long as you need to. I'll call Todd and let him know where you are." She turned out the lights and closed the door behind her.

I woke up three hours later. My caring friend had known what I needed—I had to stop to rest.

If you feel like you're always tired and not getting enough rest, you're probably not sleeping adequately. According to the Centers for Disease Control and Prevention (CDC) and the American Academy of Sleep Medicine, adults need seven or more hours of sleep per night. But more than one-third of Americans don't get enough sleep. And almost half of us have only fair or poor sleep quality, with stress keeping us awake at night.

There's a strong correlation between stress levels and the sleep cycle. Stress interferes with the amount and quality of sleep. The irony is that not getting enough sleep can make you feel more stressed. Inadequate sleep also leads to chronic health conditions and mental health disorders.

Right now, you may be thinking, *Oh great, Kristin. So I'm not sleeping and now I'm in danger of acquiring a chronic health condition?* I get it. You may find it difficult to get more rest than you already are. However, sufficient sleep must be a priority to prevent burnout, since, among other things, regular sleep helps our muscles relax and repair, our hormones regulate, and our brains recover and recharge for the next day.

Better and longer sleep has as much to do with what we do *during* the day as it does with when we lay our head down at night. To improve our sleep, we have to reduce our overall stress levels and balance caring for our mental, emotional, spiritual, and physical health. Dr. Saundra Dalton-Smith explained it this way in *Sacred Rest:* "Sleep is different from rest, but good-quality sleep trickles down from a life well rested." We can easily feel guilty for taking time for ourselves. But the more rested and healthier we are, the better parents we will be.

Here are some vital steps you can take to help improve your sleep:

During the day:

- Go outside in the sunlight or eat by a window to help reset your circadian clock.
- Engage in some type of physical activity such as walking, stretching, or strength training to reduce stress and boost your natural sleep hormones like melatonin.
- Practice an exercise of deep breathing, mindfulness, or scanning your body for tension.
- Pray, go on a prayer walk, or meditate on Scripture.

In the evening:

- Begin your bedtime ritual at approximately the same time each night.

- Turn on your phone's blue light filter and dim the room lighting.
- Avoid working or checking emails in bed and limit device use thirty minutes before bedtime.
- Do something that relaxes you like taking a hot bath or shower, diffusing a soothing oil like lavender, or drinking a warm (non-caffeinated) beverage like chamomile tea.

Before you go to sleep:

- Jot down any thoughts, tasks, or worries before you lie down.
- Do a deep-breathing or a progressive muscle relaxation exercise.
- Listen to a guided sleep meditation or calming music.
- Pray to God about your anxieties.

I encourage you to pray about ways you can improve your sleep and feel more rested. God wants you to sleep soundly, and he wants to give you the gift of providing for your family, even while you sleep. Trust him with your worries, and rest well in his peaceful presence.

Pray

Jesus, help me quiet my thoughts and relax my body. Please give me restful sleep.

Ponder 3 MINUTES

Take a few minutes to record your thoughts.

1. How might God want to help you rest better?

____

2. Identify one way you can lower your stress levels and prepare your mind and body for sleep:

During the day: _______________

In the evening: _______________

Right before bedtime: _______________

Practice 4 MINUTES

At bedtime tonight, try this calming routine to help you wind down for a better night's sleep.

1. Begin by taking two slow, deep breaths.
2. Lie down in bed and rest your head on the pillow.
3. Close your eyes. Notice how the soft mattress and warm covers feel. Your body feels heavy and is sinking into the bed.
4. Slowly scan through your body and tense and relax each muscle group from your feet to your head. Continue taking deep breaths.
5. God is there with you. Pray and release any anxieties to him and fall asleep in his peaceful presence.

Plan

Choose either daytime, evening, or right before bedtime and pick one of the following habits you wish to begin today.

1. Reduce stress levels during the day.

or

2. Establish a regular bedtime routine in the evening.

or

3. Soothe your mind and body before going to sleep.

REMEMBER

Accept God's gift of rest.

DAY 13

Refresh Your Soul

He gives me green pastures to lie in.
He leads me by calm pools of water.
He restores my strength.
—Psalm 23:2–3, ERV

I surveyed the messy kitchen, and an overflowing sink of dirty dishes and sticky counters stared back at me. My long to-do list waited on the table. I had more to accomplish than I could possibly get done before it was time to sit in the school pickup line. I stood there drained. Then I made a choice. I turned and walked out of the kitchen and traversed an obstacle course of toys through the house. I grabbed my purse on the way out the door and hopped into the car.

After driving to the park, I stepped out into the fresh air and headed toward the trailhead. I entered the woods and temporarily left my stressful day behind. Veering off the trail, I followed a narrow path to the creek and sat down on a rock. I closed my eyes and allowed my mind to flow with the soothing stream. Several scriptures came to mind, and I realized Jesus was there with me. I waited quietly, listening for him and resting in his refreshing Spirit. In that brief respite from my overwhelming day, Jesus restored my mental and emotional energy and filled me with new joy.

I didn't check off all my tasks that day. But I picked up my kids reenergized and in a pleasant mood. Like most parents, I can't simply drop my responsibilities like that very often. But even on the busiest days, I've learned how to momentarily leave my to-do list and mentally "walk down to the stream" to seek spiritual refreshment.

To reduce our stress levels, remain healthy, and parent well, we must regularly choose to rejuvenate our heart, mind, and spirit in God's Word and presence. I encourage you to schedule time to physically get outside into the fresh air to rest mentally, emotionally, and spiritually. But when you can't, take a break right where you are.

You can listen to a guided Scripture meditation that helps you use your senses to picture yourself with Jesus in a Scripture passage. This is a great way to relax while growing closer to God. Christians have practiced guided Scripture meditation throughout history. This practice is linked to significant improvements in anxiety, depression, stress levels, sleep, blood pressure, and cognition. A guided meditation will lead you in listening for Jesus to speak to you, letting him care for you, and allowing him to fill you with inner peace and fresh life.

We are spiritually thirsty people, and only a deeper relationship with Jesus can satisfy us. He is our Good Shepherd-King, and he desires to nourish us with his Word and refresh us with his Spirit. He invites us to come to him so he can make us whole again and show us how to return to our day renewed and truly alive. He wants us to flourish. In *A Shepherd Looks at Psalm 23,* W. Phillip Keller reflected on what he believed pleased his "Master's heart and mind." He wrote, "He loves to see me contented, quiet, at rest, and relaxed. He delights to know my soul and spirit have been refreshed and satisfied."

Jesus is calling to you. Are you willing to follow him off the noisy, busy road of your day and down a path to refreshing streams? He knows what you need in this moment and desires to care for you. Allow him to renew your mind, revive your body, and refresh your spirit. Close your eyes. You are there with him.

Pray

Jesus, I know you are here with me. I long to rest with you by tranquil waters and feel the wind of your refreshing Spirit.

Ponder 3 MINUTES

Take a few minutes to record your thoughts.

1. In what ways do you find it difficult to mentally leave your day to refresh your soul?

____

2. How might listening to a guided Scripture meditation or reflecting on these verses in Psalm 23 help you?

____

3. How could your spiritual refreshment benefit your family?

Practice 5 MINUTES

Come rest with Jesus.

Optional: Play flowing stream nature sounds.

1. Begin by taking two slow, deep breaths.

2. Close your eyes and picture yourself leaving your hectic day and following Jesus down to a peaceful brook.

3. Let him guide you to sit on a sun-warmed rock or soft bed of green moss on the water's edge.

4. Notice your surroundings. Feel the earth beneath you. Listen to the soothing stream gently flowing over the rocks into a still pool. You can see clear to the bottom. Take off your shoes and dip your feet in the cool water.

5. Take a deep breath and enjoy the scent of sweet-smelling grass and blooming wildflowers. Welcome the gentle breeze brushing your skin and the sunlight warming your face.

6. Rest in this serene space Jesus created for you. You are safe and loved. There's no need to say anything. He knows you're here because you desire to grow closer to him. Simply rest in his presence and allow him to fill you with fresh strength and joy.

Plan

Take a brief respite.

Pick a time today to pause and try one of these devotional practices:

1. Listen to flowing stream nature sounds. Close your eyes and sit with Jesus.
2. Read Psalm 23 and rest in God's presence.
3. Relax to a guided Scripture meditation.

REMEMBER

Follow Jesus to refreshing streams.

DAY 14

Pray in Silence

The Holy Spirit helps us in our weakness. . . . [He] prays for us with groanings that cannot be expressed in words.

—Romans 8:26

Urgent dinging startled me. I sat up in the vinyl hospital chair. Bethany Grace's shrill cry of pain pierced my heart. I lowered the bed's safety rail and searched for the source of her discomfort. She couldn't tell me where it hurt. Sometimes I know what she needs, and I can speak her unique language. But with her speech disorder, it can often be challenging to decipher what she's trying to say.

I felt her forehead, checked her back, and inspected her feet. Then I took off the soft cast protecting her IV. Redness and swelling. I paged the nurse, and she walked in.

I motioned to my daughter's arm. "Her IV site is hurting. Can you please see what can be done?"

"Oh. Yes, we're going to need to put in a new one. I'll be right back."

After the nurse finished placing a new line, Bethany Grace relaxed, and the heart rate alarm faded. I stood by her bed holding her hand as she drifted back to sleep. My heart ached. There in the heavy silence of that hospital room, I heard God's sweet Spirit whisper to mine, *I'm here with you.* He met me there and comforted me, and I hadn't even prayed a word.

As parents, we often know what our children need even before they say anything, and we can understand what they're trying to communicate in a way no one else can. But sometimes we might not know how to pray for our children or for ourselves. In more profound ways than even a parent, our heavenly Father knows and understands us—how we feel and what we're thinking—and he doesn't have to try to figure out what we need. And just as a parent advocates for their child's needs, the Holy Spirit talks to the Father for us when we can't speak for ourselves due to emotional or mental distress, spiritual struggles, or physical ailments.

When we practice the stillness of silence, we can truly experience being with the Holy Spirit. When we leave the noise and enter a silent space, we can become aware of his Spirit and hear him in the depths of our soul. Even amid struggles, mindfully bringing our awareness to God's loving Spirit can soothe our angst. When we're experiencing stress and anxiety, sitting in silent prayer helps calm our nervous system. Whether upset, lost, or confused, we can sit down and realize our need for the Spirit's healing and guidance. When we commune with the Spirit, we don't leave the same. We leave whole.

Our heavenly Father already knows what we and our children need better than we do ourselves. Before we even utter a word, he knows what we're going to say (see Psalm 139:4). We may not have the words to describe our complicated emotions or heartache for our children. But his love and healing go deeper than words. The more time we spend with Jesus and the more personally we know him, the fewer words are needed. Because sometimes words aren't even enough. Sometimes they become groans.

In *Wordless Prayer,* Tammie Southerland described Romans 8:26 like this: "In the depths of our souls, where the Spirit of God intertwines with our being, exists a profound and mysterious language of groaning . . . connecting us intimately with the heart of God."

God understands you. He knows how hard parenting can be. He feels your every struggle, your every heartache. Sometimes it may feel hard to come to him in prayer. But you don't have to try to find him. He's already there in and around you, even though you can't see him or audibly hear his voice. When you've run out of words to pray, allow the Spirit to lay his healing hands on you. Simply be present with him, within you. Trust Jesus's Spirit. He wants to pray for you and help you in ways you can't even understand.

Pray

Holy Spirit, I'm here waiting for you in this moment, and I believe you are here with me. You know what's on my heart and mind and what I need most.

Ponder 2 MINUTES

Take a few minutes to record your thoughts.

1. How do you feel about silent prayer? Do you find it uncomfortable and difficult, or comforting and natural?

2. How can you experience the Holy Spirit's presence in deeper ways?

Practice 5 MINUTES

Pray in silence.

1. Begin by taking two slow, deep breaths.
2. As you inhale, silently pray: "You know what I need."

   As you exhale, silently pray: "Help me in my weakness."
3. Take another breath.

   Inhale: "You know my family's needs."

   Exhale: "Help us in our weakness."
4. Then sit in silence. Just be in God's Spirit.
5. Notice any thoughts or emotions as they come up. Exhale and silently release them to God.

Plan

Open up a space.

Make time today to silently sit with the Holy Spirit.

REMEMBER

Listen for God's Spirit in the silence.

DAY 15

Manage Technology

Fill your minds with beauty and truth. Meditate on whatever is honorable, whatever is right, whatever is pure, whatever is lovely, whatever is good, whatever is virtuous and praiseworthy.

—Philippians 4:8, Voice

Finally, a break. I picked up my phone and became absorbed in scrolling through social media reels. When I noticed the time, twenty minutes had passed. I looked up at the kids. They were both engrossed in their devices. I had missed twenty minutes I could have spent with them instead of flipping through other people's lives. Guilt crept in. What had they been filling their minds with for the past half hour?

"What are you guys watching?" They held up their screens. *Babies giggling. Okay, that's not bad. And videos of teens pulling pranks. Not terrible, I guess.*

Their screens drew their faces back down. I realized I hadn't set a timer for screen time. I knew I was about to spark a battle. "Come help me make dinner. It's time for a screen break."

"Mama! No! A little longer."

I held my ground, and we eventually made it to the kitchen, all of us in a grumpy mood.

A whopping 86 percent of Americans say they are constantly attached to their phones and frequently check their emails, texts, and social media accounts. The increasing amount of time we spend on devices is harming our physical health, mental health, and family bonds. The use of smartphones directly increases stress, anxiety, and depression. The psychological term for this condition is "technostress."

The temptation to pick up our phones is strong, even addictive. Many Americans live mindlessly, chronically distracted by devices. Technology has made us always available to others who expect us to respond quickly. When we're constantly checking our devices, it's nearly impossible to live mindfully. We aren't fully mentally there in the moment, since the ding of notifications pulls us out of our conversations with others.

When it comes to parents, nearly half say they feel disconnected from their families, even when they're together, due to technology. Being distracted by our phones interferes with parenting mindfully and connecting with our children, which causes added stress. If you feel like your electronic devices are managing you instead of the other way around, it's time to reclaim control. Reducing household screen time can significantly improve your and your family's well-being. After just two weeks of limiting internet use, 91 percent of adults said they felt better, and 71 percent reported significant reduction in depression and anxiety symptoms.

As you try this out for yourself, remember to start small. Take a ten-minute technology break today. Work up to longer periods like a half day or even a full day when you can unplug as a family. Reducing screen time will allow you to spend that time in different ways—talking to one another, resting, or enjoying an activity together.

Technology does enhance our lives. But at the point it stops serving us, screens have become our master. Serving God is no longer our focus. In *Stronger Than Stress,* Barb Roose asked: "How much of our stress response is because of shrinking our view of God and trying to fit Him into our small-screen perspective?"

The more time we spend looking at screens, the more mental energy we waste trying to filter out the bad—the lies, unwholesome images and talk, discord, violence, and injustice. Upsetting images cause us stress and can even disturb our sleep. What occupies our time and attention influences our thoughts, emotions, words, and actions. Instead, Jesus calls us to center our thoughts on him.

The following questions may help as you consider how to spend time on your devices:

- Is this site, video, or activity worthy of my time?
- Are these images filling me with darkness or light?
- Does watching this bring me peace or more stress?
- Is this message sowing love or fear and hate?
- What eternal value does this have?

As you ask yourself these questions, try to listen for the Holy Spirit and see if he will whisper his answers to your heart. God wants to fill your mind with good and beautiful words of truth based on his Word that will help you fall deeper in love with him and help you love others more. Listen for his nudging to put down your phone and look up.

Pray

Jesus, forgive me for the times I've allowed technology and social media to rule me. Help me limit my time online and center my thoughts on images and words that please you.

Ponder 2 MINUTES

Take a few minutes to record your thoughts.

1. Name one way technology is causing you and your children more stress.

2. What is one step you can take to better manage technology use?

Practice 4 MINUTES

1. Begin by taking two slow, deep breaths.
2. Reflect on all the ways you use technology throughout your day.
3. Close your eyes and picture the images and messages that infiltrate your mind.
4. Pray: "Jesus, please show me the ways I fill my mind that please you and the ways my devices help or hinder my relationship with my child and with you."
5. Now imagine one way you will modify your device use.

Plan

Begin to reduce your screen time.

Plan a daily twenty-minute technology break.

You may also choose to:

1. Turn off notifications for social media, email, news, and ads.
2. Track your screen time.

3. Set time limits for apps.

4. Plan a half-day or daylong digital detox.

REMEMBER

Fill your mind with good, true, and beautiful images.

Part 4

Embracing Your Worth

DAY 16

Lay Down Perfectionism

There is no one on earth who does what is right all the time and never makes a mistake.

—Ecclesiastes 7:20, GNT

We all marched out of our bedrooms like the penguins on our holiday pajamas.

"Okay. Over here in front of the tree."

Even though last year's Christmas photo session had ended in several of us crying, I was hoping to finally get the perfect family picture this year.

"Mama, do we *have* to do this?"

"Yes. I want to get a family photo. Please help, and we'll get done faster." I set the timer and ran to my spot. "Look at the camera. Everyone smile."

Twenty minutes of bickering and thirty takes later, I flipped through the candid shots of blurry heads tilted all directions, talking mouths, and unhappy stares. *How hard can it be to take a good picture?*

My frustration and disappointment dampened the morning with my family. Later in the day, I scrolled through the photos again. We all looked miserable. *Why is this so important to me? To have a memento in an album on the bookshelf? To have an image to post on social media? To feel good about myself as a mom?* I realized the answers were yes, yes, and yes. That was the last year we had Mama's required Christmas morning photo session.

I'm a recovering perfectionist. I get these ideas in my head about how things have to be, and I feel a compulsion to do things just right. Even now, I have to recognize this tendency and work through it. I used to exhaust myself keeping the house immaculate, trying to be a perfect wife and mom, and going above and beyond at work. During my long mental health recovery, I learned that perfection is an illusion. It's unattainable. If I allowed perfection to remain my goal, I would always be following a mirage, chasing disappointment, and dragging behind me the weight of self-criticism.

Perfectionists experience higher levels of stress, depression, and anxiety. There are two parts to perfectionism:

1. Setting and striving for high personal expectations and standards

2. Being overly self-critical and chronically concerned with others' criticism and approval

Brené Brown, an expert on the topic, explained it this way in *The Gifts of Imperfection:* "Healthy striving is self-focused—*How can I improve?* Perfectionism is other-focused—*What will they think?*"

I still put too much pressure on myself, but now I have become more aware of these moments and can challenge my unhealthy thought patterns. I'm more easygoing and happier. And so is my family. We can still have high standards for ourselves and strive to be better people, parents, or employees—but with balance and grace. A healthy solution is to revise our expectations for ourselves, our children, and others into more reasonable and relevant goals.

Now when considering my work, tasks, or parenting, I often ask myself, "Is this good enough for now?" I strive to be a "good enough" parent. Pediatrician and psychoanalyst D. W. Winnicott first introduced the theory of the "good enough mother," which has since evolved to the concept of "good enough parenting." Good enough parents care for their children's emotional, physical, and psychological needs in a sensitive and responsive way . . . but not perfectly. This parenting approach is actually better for a child's health and development than constantly trying to care for every single need. There's no such thing as a perfect parent. Not even close. Trying to be perfect actually makes us less effective.

Once I understood that only God is perfect, I realized that if I thought I could be perfect all the time this side of heaven, then what I was really trying to do was be God. Oh, how this freed me! God doesn't expect you to be perfect either, because you can't be. You're human, and only he is God. Embrace and celebrate the liberation from the shackles of unreasonable expectations. It's time for us to let go of perfectionism and discover a life of freedom and joy.

Pray

Jesus, I know only you are perfect, and you don't ask me to be. Teach me the difference between doing my best and working too hard.

Ponder 3 MINUTES

Take a few minutes to record your thoughts.

1. In what ways do you put pressure on yourself to achieve high standards?

---

2. What is one aspect of life or type of project you may work harder and longer on than is actually necessary?

---

3. Name one perfectionistic tendency you can let go of to free up more time and emotional energy.

Practice 4 MINUTES

Measure your expectations.

1. Begin by taking two slow, deep breaths.

2. Picture yourself overdoing it on one of the projects or tasks you identified in the Ponder section.

3. What thoughts come up?

4. How do you feel inside your body?

5. Notice any emotions you're feeling.

6. On a scale of 1 to 10 (with 1 being no pressure and 10 being extreme pressure), how would you rate the amount of stress you're experiencing?

7. What is an appropriate and healthy goal for this task?

Plan

Challenge perfectionism.

The next time you notice yourself working really hard on a project or pushing yourself to do better, pause and ask yourself:

1. Are my expectations reasonable and what's needed for this task?

2. Is what I've already done good enough?

3. How can I move forward in a healthy way?

REMEMBER

Let go of trying to be perfect.

DAY 17

Trade Busyness for Simplicity

The Lord said to her, "My dear Martha, you are worried and upset over all these details! There is only one thing worth being concerned about. Mary has discovered it, and it will not be taken away from her."

—Luke 10:41–42

I carefully placed the 1 and 5 candles on the three-tier ice castle cake. *Just in time.* After two days of baking and decorating, I felt like I had just completed a competition on a television bake-off show.

Bethany Grace's eyes sparkled like the sequins on her princess gown and the ice-blue jewels in her crown. The elaborate shimmering decorations made me feel like I was in a winter wonderland. I scurried around serving lunch to the other children and parents, making sure they were having fun. Then it was time for the princess character to lead the singing. The room was so crowded, I became trapped on the other side and was unable to get around to be next to Bethany Grace for the big moment. She looked around for me.

"Happy birthday, dear B-e-t-h-a-n-y, happy birthday to you."

That's when I noticed it. The tiara had loosened Bethany Grace's hair, and her bangs had fallen around her face. I'd been so busy, I hadn't seen it. And now it was quickly becoming too late. I watched in horror as she leaned forward, her hair dangling in the lit candles. By a miracle, the flames extinguished just in time.

I have a history of overdoing things. For the longest time, I struggled with never feeling good enough and believed I had to work to earn the approval I so desperately craved. I wasted so much energy fretting over meaningless details that ultimately really didn't matter, especially from an eternal perspective.

If this sounds familiar, you're not alone. Our society pushes busyness, especially on parents. The result: burnout. The added stress from doing more than necessary strains our mental health and family's well-being. Parenting and family burnout also spills over to burnout at work, and work stress adds to parenting burnout.

How can we counteract the toxicity of busyness? One way is to embrace simplicity. To shift from the urge to be constantly *doing* to simply *being* in the present moment. If we can find ways to eliminate unnecessary projects and simplify others, we will reduce stress and create a space for what truly matters. This means prioritizing our values and defying society's pressure to devote ourselves to constant work and productivity.

As I became more aware of the unnecessary weight I was constantly shouldering in my own life, I began to ask myself, Who is this really going to make a difference to a year from now? That question has helped me limit the amount of pressure and responsibility I place on myself. Sometimes I still succumb to our society's prized busyness sickness, as I did with my daughter's fifteenth birthday party. But for most birthdays, I follow wise advice another mom gave me years ago: "Go simple. Get a pizza, buy a cake, invite two or three friends, go to a park, and enjoy your time together."

So, when are we doing too much? Wanda E. Brunstetter makes it simple: "If you are too busy to pray, you are busier than God wants you to be." In today's Scripture passage, Martha was concerned about showing her devotion to Jesus by preparing a big meal and being a good hostess. But while fussing over all the details she thought were most important, she stayed too busy to spend time with Jesus. He just wanted her to sit at his feet and listen to his teaching and know him better like her sister Mary was doing. Mary had chosen what was most important and discovered the best part of the meal: simply being with Jesus. Teresa of Avila wisely said, "The closer one approaches to God, the simpler one becomes."

All God wants is a relationship with us. When we rest in his presence, we don't need to find our sense of identity in our productivity. When we know who we are in Jesus (unconditionally accepted, loved, and forgiven), we don't have to try to earn our merit through our accomplishments. When we pause to simply *be* with Jesus, he lifts the weighted cloak of stress and anxiety off our shoulders and wraps us in the silk shawl of his peace.

Your worth isn't based on how good a parent you are, how often your boss praises you, or how much you do for others. Tune out the lie that your value comes from doing more. Your worth is found in your relationship with Jesus, and your identity comes from *simply being* God's beloved child. You are enough before you ever do anything. Cultivate simplicity and break free from the bondage of busyness. Choose to sit at Jesus's feet—learning to love him more and know him better—and discover the best part.

Pray

Jesus, I come to sit at your feet and learn. Show me ways I overdo things. Help me understand that my worth and identity are in knowing you and living in your unconditional love, mercy, and grace.

Ponder 2 MINUTES

Take a few minutes to record your thoughts.

1. What are some unnecessary tasks or details you could cut out?

2. How might having a deeper understanding of your identity in God change your inner drive to do more?

Practice 4 MINUTES

Just be.

1. Begin by taking two slow, deep breaths.

2. Close your eyes and imagine sharing a meal with Jesus.

3. Listen to him speaking *to you:*

"You don't need to do anything to earn my love. Your worth is in your relationship with me."

4. Picture yourself sitting at the table in silence, simply being in his presence.

Plan

1. Choose one task you can eliminate or scale back on.

2. As you decide to simplify your life in this way, pray:

Jesus, I know my worth is not in this task.
My identity is in you.

REMEMBER

Choose simplicity and discover the best part—knowing Jesus.

DAY 18

Give Yourself Compassion

As God's chosen people, holy and dearly loved, clothe yourselves with compassion, kindness, humility, gentleness and patience.

—Colossians 3:12, NIV

I tried to catch my breath as I waited at the counter. The receptionist finally looked up. "Can I help you?"

"Yes, please. My daughter has an appointment. I apologize; we're running a little late."

I watched as she pecked on the computer keyboard. I really hoped we wouldn't have to reschedule after all we had gone through to get here.

The receptionist scrunched up her face. *Peck. Peck. Peck.* She cocked her head to one side. Then her eyes widened. "You sure are late! Her appointment was yesterday."

"What? I'm sorry. Are you sure? Is there any way we can still see the doctor today?"

"Yes, I'm sure. And no. You're going to have to reschedule. Let's see . . . her next available is in three months."

How had I messed this up? This was a really important appointment.

As we walked back to the parking garage, I replayed my hectic week over and over in my head. Each time I rehashed the events leading up to my goof, I grew more self-compassionate. Before pulling out of the parking garage, I actually comforted and encouraged myself.

Kristin, she has so many appointments. It's amazing this doesn't happen more often. You're a good mom, and you're doing an amazing job. It'll be okay.

My entire life, I've expected more from myself than I have from any other person. When I became a mom, my self-demands intensified. I chastised myself for making mistakes and not doing as well as I thought I should. This self-induced pressure steadily built until I imploded.

Self-criticism, the second half of perfectionism along with setting very high personal standards and goals, is linked to lower overall well-being. When we criticize ourselves, we activate our body's stress response system, which makes us more reactive to everyday hassles. Harsh self-scrutiny and worrying about how others see us add fuel to our stress and mental health strain, making it more likely we will develop anxiety and depression.

The healthy solution is to practice self-compassion—cheerleading ourselves through our challenges. Self-compassion involves caring for ourselves emotionally and being sympathetic to our own pain and struggles. We respect and appreciate who we are and are better able to offer ourselves grace. When we're compassionate toward ourselves, we become resilient, calmer, and more effective. Being self-compassionate helps us to respond less out of our own emotions, guilt, and self-doubt so we can better meet our children's needs.

Dr. Kristin Neff and Dr. Christopher Germer are world-renowned psychologists and pioneers in the field of self-compassion research. They wrote, "Self-compassion is pretty straightforward—it's simply compassion turned inward. When we're self-compassionate, we give ourselves the same kindness, care, concern, and help when we struggle that we typically give to others. We're warm and understanding rather than cold and judgmental when things are challenging in our lives."

To extend yourself compassion:

1. Be kind to yourself: Talk to yourself in a supportive and soothing tone like you would for a hurting friend.
2. Remember you're human: Recognize the fact that all people fail, make mistakes, and feel inadequate at times.
3. Be mindful: Become aware of your emotions and the situation in the present moment and take a balanced perspective.

One way to practice self-compassion is to rephrase critical messages with more objective and kinder self-statements. For example, instead of saying "I should have been helping my child more," say "I helped as much as I could with all the responsibilities I've had."

Recognizing we're human just like everyone else will help us connect with others rather than isolate in guilt and shame. I imagine it saddens Jesus to watch us be mean to ourselves and hide from others. When we treat ourselves with loving-kindness, we are better able to love and care for others. It is in and through God's all-encompassing love for us that we are truly able to show ourselves and others compassion, grace, and mercy. You are God's dearly beloved. Be gentle and patient with yourself as Jesus tenderly embraces you in his loving arms.

Pray

Jesus, open my ears to hear the ways I speak to myself unlovingly. Lift my face to see your compassionate gaze. Free my heart and mind to know your loving thoughts toward me.

Ponder 2 MINUTES

Take a few minutes to record your thoughts.

1. List any self-critical statements you sometimes find yourself thinking.

2. How might you extend yourself kindness and compassion in those situations?

Practice 4 MINUTES

Center your heart on Jesus's loving-kindness.

1. Begin by taking two slow, deep breaths.
2. Pray:

May I embrace your tender compassion for me in my struggles and pain.
Help me be gentle and kind to myself when I think I should do better.

May I understand my worth is not tied to how well I do.
Help me accept that I make mistakes and fail like everyone else.

May I experience your unconditional love for me, even in my flaws.
Help me love and care for others like you cherish and comfort me.

Amen.

Plan

Speak loving-kindness to yourself.

1. Choose one line from today's prayer and memorize it.
2. Look in the mirror and recite it while you get ready for bed and then again in the morning.

REMEMBER

Be kind and compassionate to yourself.

DAY 19

Replace Comparison with Confidence

In his grace, God has given us different gifts for doing certain things well.

—Romans 12:6

"I'm going to show you how to prep these three healthy meals your whole family will love."

The mom's kitchen sparkled behind her. She stood behind the huge granite island lined with fresh ingredients and empty freezer bags.

How does she have the time?

I scrolled. Another bubbly mom stood in her shiny kitchen and showed off the small containers lining her countertop. "As a mom of five, I'm prepping fresh snacks for the entire week." Various dips and cute animal faces shaped from fruits and cheeses waited for her children's eager fingers.

I can barely get to the grocery store.

I flipped to the next reel.

"Use these three homeschooling tips to better support your children in their learning."

I was never able to homeschool. I'm just not made that way.

I dropped my phone on the couch and sighed. Suddenly, all the aspects of parenting I struggle with ganged up on me. *Why can't you get it all done?* My insecurities heckled me until I ended up emotionally deflated.

I know I'm not naturally gifted in many aspects of parenting. I sometimes watch how-to videos to get ideas and improve my skills in those areas. But my eagerness to learn can quickly turn into comparison. Sometimes when I watch other parents, I feel inadequate and my confidence and joy begin to fade.

It can be helpful to learn how to improve our existing strengths and maybe even grow in ways we feel we could use some help. But when we find ourselves feeling bad and overwhelmed, scrolling online is no longer healthy or helpful.

Comparing ourselves to other parents can cause feelings of inadequacy and can increase the internal pressure to measure up to others' standards and successes. Results of one large study concluded that "the expectations of Western societies may be so demanding that some parents might feel that they are never doing enough for their children and that they must constantly try harder to become more perfect parents and have better children." Evaluating ourselves based on what other parents are doing on social media can make us feel even more like we can't fulfill all our responsibilities and that we are less competent as parents. When we compare our parenting to others' on social media, we have 51 percent greater odds of developing depression symptoms. But we need to remember that the images we see of most parents on social media are often one-sided; they're showing off their natural parenting talents, not the areas in which they struggle.

Not all parents and kids are created the same, and God has different plans and purposes for each unique family. This is his special design. In his lavish grace, he gives each parent different spiritual gifts and parenting abilities. He wants you to develop *your* unique gifts so you can best love *your* child, who has distinct characteristics and needs. Your Creator has a personalized plan for your life. He wants you to grow and use those skills he has given you to fulfill your purpose. If you remain stuck in focusing on everyone else's natural abilities, you'll miss the beauty and joy of watching how God can use your own gifts.

Heather Creekmore reminded us, "Every minute you spend comparing is time stolen from your pursuit of God's plans for you." God has gifted you in certain parenting abilities. If your parenting strengths don't quickly come to mind, reflect and ask God to show you what they are. Because you *do* have spiritual gifts and natural parenting abilities. And you likely have more you haven't even discovered yet. So replace comparison with confidence in who God has specially created you to be and the ways in which he has equipped you to love others best.

Pray

God, thank you for the parenting abilities you have given me. Help me discover and better develop my gifts. I look to you for my confidence and ask you to fulfill your plan and purpose for my life.

Ponder 2 MINUTES

Take a few minutes to record your thoughts.

1. In what areas do you compare yourself to other parents?

---

2. What are two of your parenting gifts or strengths?

Practice 3 MINUTES

Thank God for your parenting gifts.

1. Begin by taking two slow, deep breaths.

   As you inhale, pray: *In your grace*

   Exhale: *you gave me gifts.*

2. This time pray:

   Inhale: *Lord, thank you*

   Exhale: *for my gift of* ______________________.

3. Repeat this breath prayer for any other gifts that come to mind.

Plan

Remember your gifts.

1. The next time you notice you're comparing yourself to someone else, pause and observe your thoughts and emotions.
2. Thank God for the parenting abilities he has given you.
3. Be confident in the person God uniquely designed you to be.

REMEMBER

Replace comparison with confidence in your unique gifts.

DAY 20

Embrace Your Flaws

[The Lord] said to me, "My grace is enough for you. When you are weak, my power is made perfect in you." So I am very happy to brag about my weaknesses. Then Christ's power can live in me.

—2 Corinthians 12:9, NCV

I rushed into the restroom stall and locked the door. My heart raced. Sweat streamed down my forehead, streaking my makeup.

I can't do this. I'm terrible at interviews. Maybe I'm not even qualified.

I had prepared for weeks to secure this competitive position at a prestigious hospital. But images from my last bungled interview now paralyzed me. I stood frozen. Then a ridiculous idea popped into my head. I had read that standing in a Superman pose for two minutes can make you feel more confident and composed. Apparently, this trick reverses certain hormones in your body, lowers stress, and makes you feel like you're about to win.

I was desperate. I had worked so hard to get to this point, sacrificing time with my husband and elementary-aged children. So, as silly as I felt, I took a wide stance, bent my elbows, and put my hands on my hips. I hummed the Superman theme song in my head: "Duh-duh-duh." Then I raised my arms above my head and flexed my muscles. I didn't hear anyone else in the bathroom, so I whispered out loud, "Duh-duh-duh!"

I stepped out and smiled in the mirror. *God, please help me do well, despite any lingering insecurities. Be my strength and speak through me.* Then I walked into the conference room and rocked that interview.

Our human nature pushes us to strive to be self-sufficient. Many people believe that admitting their weaknesses would be self-defeating and ineffective. Failure can make us feel small and inadequate, especially as parents. So we work hard to provide for our families and care for their needs. When we fall short, we can feel like we've failed our children.

But we don't have to continue struggling through our inadequacies. When we accept our imperfections, we actually experience less stress and greater mental and emotional health, resiliency, and contentment. But we have to first accept our shortcomings and recognize the areas in which we could be stronger before we can grow.

From a faith perspective, when we embrace our weaknesses, we recognize our need for God. We open a space for him to come in and fill every part of us. He helps us thrive in our challenges and become the best version of ourselves. If we had no deficiencies, then there would be no room for Jesus's power in our lives. When we experience the gift of his extravagant grace, we want to do the opposite of what our culture rewards. Instead of trying to hide our imperfections, we boldly claim them because they reveal the amazing things God has done in our lives.

I no longer want to try to be perfect. I want to appreciate the gift of my limitations and the blessings that come from my imperfections. Oh, how wonderful are my inadequacies! Through my weaknesses and mistakes, God has accomplished more in ways I never could have imagined. "Now I am glad to boast about how weak I am; I am glad to be a living demonstration of Christ's power, instead of showing off my own power and abilities" (2 Corinthians 12:9, TLB). When our abilities are insufficient, his grace is abundant. When we admit our need for God's help, his response is amazing. Where there's a weakness, there's an opportunity for a fantastic showing of God's marvelous grace, deep spiritual growth, and a powerful impact in others' lives.

God uses our flaws as opportunities to display his magnificent love and special plan in our lives. But we must fully embrace our weaknesses to fully receive his power. Then and only then can God do his beautiful work in us.

So offer your inadequacies to Jesus. Give him your exhaustion from trying to do everything in your own strength. Look to him, throw up your hands, and say, "I don't know how to do this, Lord. I'm weak. Will you help me?" Then enjoy watching him do the amazing and unexpected in your life.

Pray

Jesus, thank you for the gift of your lavish grace. Take my flaws and failures, and perfect your marvelous work in me. Show your splendor through my life.

Ponder 3 MINUTES

Take a few minutes to record your thoughts.

1. List any areas of your life in which you feel stuck, inadequate, or weak.

---

2. Pick one weakness with which you struggle. What would it be like to ask God for help?

Practice 5 MINUTES

Offer your weaknesses to Jesus.

1. Begin by taking two slow, deep breaths.
2. Picture yourself struggling with a particular weakness.
3. Reflect on these questions:

   What's happening?

   How do you feel in your body?

   What are you thinking and feeling?

4. Jesus is there with you. Look up at him and lift your hands.

5. Offer this prayer:

Jesus, I'm weak in ______________________. Your grace is more than enough.

Jesus, I'm imperfect at ______________________. Perfect your power in me.

Plan

Rejoice in your inadequacies.

The next time you find yourself having difficulty with a situation or task:

1. Look to Jesus and say, "I'm weak in this area. Will you help me and fill me with your strength and power?"
2. Watch what God does next and tell others what he's done in your life.

REMEMBER

Embrace your flaws so God can work through you.

Part 5

Drawing Closer to Jesus

DAY 21

Trust Your Wonderful Counselor

Pour out your heart to him,
for God is our refuge.
—Psalm 62:8

I finished steeping my tea bag, then we stepped into her office. As I sank into the plush sofa, I smiled at my trusted counselor. I felt safe with her.

She smiled back. "What's on your mind today?"

I cradled the hot paper cup in my hands. The warmth comforted me. "I'm not sure what to think about . . ."

She leaned in a bit. "What thought's troubling you the most?"

"I'm struggling." I looked down. "I just feel overwhelmed."

Her tone softened. "Tell me about what's going on. Has something happened?"

"It's been a rough couple of days. I had a stressful meeting with the school, then Bethany Grace ended up in an ambulance, Todd and I had a fight, and I've had to battle with insurance."

My therapist sat up straight. "You've been through a lot. I've had to hold on to my seat just hearing about your roller-coaster week."

"I'm tired of dealing with all this. I feel bad for wishing things were different."

"That Bethany Grace didn't have all those needs?"

"Yes. I guess so." Somehow her saying it first made it easier for me to admit it.

"Kristin, your feelings are what make you human, and keeping them a secret is what can prevent you from being healthy. Has it helped talking about it?"

"Yes. I do feel better after telling you."

"Thank you for sharing with me. I'm glad you feel like you can trust me."

Confiding in someone we trust and who will listen to us sympathetically and nonjudgmentally is cathartic—it gives us an emotional release, which is necessary for our health. Whether it's a friend, church small group, spouse, family member, pastor, or counselor, talking with someone else about our problems improves our mental health and well-being. Yet the American Psychological Association reports that over half of adults feel like they don't have someone they can turn to for support in coping with their stress, they don't want to burden others with their problems, and/or other people in their lives just expect them to get over their stress on their own. It's no wonder we're stressed more than ever and our country is facing a mental health crisis. Especially as parents, we need others with whom we can share our challenges with our children. Having these trusted friends and confidantes can help remind us we're not the only ones struggling.

Sharing our personal problems with someone supportive in a high-quality relationship reduces our stress levels and can even lower our blood pressure and heart rate reactivity. Talking with someone we trust makes us feel heard, understood, and more connected. The most important aspect of sharing your personal thoughts and feelings with a friend or therapist is having a safe relationship. If you don't feel like you have someone you can confide in, consider joining a support group, speaking to a trusted pastor or counselor, or reaching out to make a new friend or reconnect with an old one.

God comforts us, speaks to us, and strengthens us through others. But other people can only help us heal to a degree. They can only touch our souls so deep. To be healthy, we need to pour out our hearts to the greatest Counselor, Jesus. As Dallas Willard wrote, "It is simply not within human capacity to care effectively for others in the depths of their life and being. . . . [God] is able to penetrate and intertwine himself within the fibers of the human self in such a way that those who are enveloped in his loving companionship will never be alone."

Jesus is your Wonderful Counselor. You can fully trust him and know he accepts you unconditionally. Even as you share your most intimate thoughts with him, you can realize that he already knows everything on your mind and heart. You can always step into his presence and lay your soul bare. He will go as deep as you are willing to go. You can feel secure and confident in him. His presence is a safe haven for you. Pour out your heart to him and hear his tender voice answering in the depths of your soul.

Pray

Jesus, thank you for bringing me comfort and counsel through others. I know you are here, that I can fully trust you with my secret thoughts, and that you accept me without condition.

Ponder 3 MINUTES

Take a few minutes to record your thoughts.

1. Who is someone trustworthy with whom you can share your thoughts and feelings and parenting struggles?

2. If you don't have someone you can confide in, how might you develop a relationship with someone?

3. What is something you're afraid to tell others?

Practice 5 MINUTES

Meet with your Counselor.

1. Begin by taking two slow, deep breaths.

2. Close your eyes and imagine sitting on a bench in a quiet courtyard. Jesus is sitting next to you.

3. This is a private and safe place.

4. What do you find here? What are those hidden thoughts you've been afraid to share with anyone else?

5. Pour out your heart to Jesus. Talk to him about your struggles and those hidden thoughts and emotions. Breathe in his unconditional acceptance and exhale your cares.

Plan

Talk to someone.

1. Set a time to connect with someone you can talk to or take a step to develop a relationship with a friend or counselor.

2. Check in with God throughout your day to share what's on your heart.

REMEMBER

Pour out your heart to your Wonderful Counselor.

DAY 22

Have a Good Cry

The LORD is close to the brokenhearted
and saves those who are crushed in spirit.

—Psalm 34:18, NIV

Suffocating dread filled the room. The doctor finally walked in. "The baby has a severe genetic disorder called cri du chat syndrome. She probably won't make it through the delivery."

I looked away. Todd scooted closer to me, squeezing my hand.

"If by some miracle the baby does survive, she'll be born with a severe heart defect and any number of medical problems. She'll be on a ventilator and will be profoundly intellectually disabled and will likely never walk or talk."

Devastation spread through every fiber of my being. Nausea squeezed my gut, and the room closed in. *Oh God, I can't breathe. Help me breathe.*

We drove home, and I collapsed onto the bed sobbing, my heart shattered. Within a couple of days, shock dried up my tears. Then disillusionment with God began to eat at my spirit. Why had he taken a healthy baby from us? How could he possibly be good and allow this to happen? I stopped praying. For two years, I refused to trust Jesus. My separation from God agonized my soul.

Then one morning, I left the house and hiked to a nearby lake. I sat down in the comforting sunlight and watched the rays sparkle on the aqua glass. I couldn't hold it in any longer.

"Jesus, I need you. I don't understand. But I'm choosing to trust you. I believe you are good."

Suddenly, I felt him closer to me than I ever had before. The tears I had held back for so long began to flow. Jesus held me as I grieved, and I gave in to his healing embrace. His Spirit revived me with fresh peace and joy.

We all experience grief at some point. Sometimes our losses are mild. Other days the pain is so intense we feel like we can't go on. Perhaps you're mourning the loss of a loved one—a parent, a sibling, a spouse, or even a child. You may be grieving for your living children at different stages. Watching our children struggle socially, medically, developmentally, spiritually, in school, in their mental health, or with substance abuse can make us heartsick. Maybe your child has a disability. Special needs parents experience chronic grief throughout their child's life, and parents of children with a terminal illness also experience anticipatory grief.

We can feel guilty about crying and experiencing negative emotions. We might believe others think we shouldn't be feeling a certain way. Even other parents might not be able to empathize with our problems or with how much it hurts to see our children deal with particular issues. We may have a difficult time allowing ourselves to feel and express our emotions. We might avoid crying or being vulnerable with others. But allowing our emotions to intensify with no release valve will keep our bodies stuck in the stress cycle and prevent us from experiencing positive emotions as well.

Having a good cry and allowing ourselves to feel all our emotions relieves stress and helps us self-soothe our bodies and minds. This is especially true when we cry with others. In addition to lowering stress, crying also releases hormones that help improve pain, dispel toxins, and enhance mood. You may feel like you can't cry or don't know how to. If that's you, begin by simply saying: "It hurts that ______________" or "I feel sad because ______________." Then sit with your thoughts and feelings and allow your emotions to surface.

When we're going through a difficult time, it can be hard to believe that God is there with us in our grief. But he is closer than you think. He is sitting right there next to you, holding you in your heartache, and experiencing every one of your tears in his great compassion.

Pain opens a door to a deeper connection with Jesus. You can be vulnerable with him. Just as he created every raindrop uniquely, Jesus knows your every tear. King David composed this melody to the Lord: "You keep track of all my sorrows. You have collected all my tears in your bottle. You have recorded each one in your book" (Psalm 56:8).

Trust Jesus with your tears. Release your emotions and cry with him. Let him console you in his welcoming arms.

Pray

Jesus, I give in to your loving embrace. You feel every tear I cry and always know why. I trust you with my pain.

Ponder 3 MINUTES

Take a few minutes to record your thoughts.

1. Describe a time you were hurting and felt far away from God.

---

2. Why do you think you were unable to draw close to Jesus during that time?

---

3. Name a painful situation you are currently experiencing.

Practice 5 MINUTES

Cry with Jesus.

1. Begin by taking two slow, deep breaths.
2. Close your eyes and think about what is causing you heartache.

3. Jesus is here with you. Compassion and concern fill his eyes.

4. Release your pain by praying these words: "Jesus, I'm hurting because ___________________."

5. Allow yourself to feel. It's okay to cry. Let Jesus comfort you in his arms.

Plan

Allow yourself to feel.

1. Notice two more emotions that arise today (whether pleasant or painful).

2. Take a moment to name and experience your feelings.

3. Welcome any tears, whether joyful or sad, and share them with Jesus.

REMEMBER

Trust Jesus with your tears.

DAY 23

Find True Contentment

Take delight in the LORD,
and he will give you your heart's desires.
—Psalm 37:4

"You have to isolate immediately."

I studied our trusted pediatrician's face. "What do you mean?"

"If Bethany Grace gets the virus, she probably won't survive. Remind me what you do for work?"

I imagined my next shift, walking into different emergency departments, homes, and jails. *I'm going to have to quit my job.* "I'm a crisis counselor."

His serious expression confirmed my fears. "And she will need to attend school at home. I'm sorry. We have to protect her."

I left feeling lost in a fog of stress. This news was just the beginning of the COVID-19 pandemic thwarting my plans for my family and my career. I had labored eight years to complete my degree and accrue clinical hours for my next license. But in 2020, all of that had to be set aside.

With a lot of spare hours on my hands, I began to spend more time praying and journaling. I soon discovered new joy in this time with God.

Lord, what do I do now? We need the money, and I love working. I waited in silence.

"Write." From deep within my being, this whisper rose.

Write? I hadn't written anything in nine years, even though my unfinished book had been tugging at my heart. So I began to type, and passion sparked. Then I received unexpected invitations to speak, which I never dreamed I'd enjoy. As I spent time seeking God for my joy, meaning, and purpose, he unveiled and fulfilled my deepest passions.

Setting goals and pursuing aspirations play essential parts in making meaning and purpose in life. Fulfilling our ambitions can be good, particularly intrinsic aims such as prioritizing personal growth, close relationships, community involvement, and physical health. Investing in self-transcendent aspirations such as helping others especially enriches our lives. However, extrinsic ambitions like focusing on popularity, financial gain, a successful image, and material possessions are linked to more dissatisfaction in life.

The higher our standards and the more we strive for in our search for contentment, the greater stress we put on ourselves. The more complex we make our lives, the more we increase the pressure and the likelihood that we'll be frustrated and disappointed when we don't reach our goals. Our hopes, plans, and dreams for our families, children, marriages, careers, and lifestyle may not be realized. Being a parent may not fully satisfy us in the ways we thought it would. That's why our contentment and peace cannot be dependent on the fulfillment of our goals and plans. True, lasting contentment only comes from growing closer to God. Scientific research even confirms what we already know. People who regularly spend time growing closer to God in prayer, singing worship songs, and reading Scripture enjoy life more.

We have so many dreams and desires. But our deepest longings really boil down to only one true yearning—our need to know *the One.* We will never find contentment when we try to grasp it for ourselves. It is in simply seeking our happiness in God that he fulfills the deepest wishes of our hearts. As Saint Augustine prayed, "For Thou hast made us for Thyself and our hearts are restless til they rest in Thee." Only God can satisfy that thirst we can't seem to quench.

When we realize that our deepest desire is to know our Creator, we discover our passions, gifts, and purpose. Our hearts begin to burn, and our spirits come alive. We experience his love and want to love him more deeply. We become lost in his wondrous depths, and what we thought we wanted fades away in his glorious beauty.

God knows the secret desires of your heart better than you do yourself. Only your Creator can give you what you really seek and what will complete you—himself. Only Jesus can satisfy your deepest yearnings. All he wants is your heart and for you to enjoy a close relationship with him. Take delight in him, and he will give you real contentment and enjoyment in life.

Pray

Jesus, you are my true desire, and I'm longing for your heart. You are the depths I seek and the love I search for. I know only you can fulfill my passions and dreams.

Ponder 2 MINUTES

Take a few minutes to record your thoughts.

1. What makes you feel closer to God? Maybe it's being outside, singing a worship song, reading Scripture, or journaling your prayers.

---

2. To what part of your day could you add in this practice?

Practice 4 MINUTES

Meditate on Psalm 37:4.

1. Begin by taking two slow, deep breaths.
2. Invite Jesus into this moment with you.

3. Focus your attention on Psalm 37:4: "Take delight in the LORD, and he will give you your heart's desires."

4. Pray: "I delight in you, Lord, the giver of my heart's desires."

5. Rest here a moment, meditating on these words.

Plan

Enjoy time with God.

Pick a time today to do one of the activities that makes you feel closer to God.

REMEMBER

Delight yourself in the One who grants your heart's desires.

DAY 24

Grow Your Joy

In your presence there is fullness of joy.

—Psalm 16:11, ESV

I screeched into the driveway after a hectic morning of dropping off the kids. A deep crease had parked itself between my brows. Stress oozed from my pores. I juggled my purse and mug as I unlocked the back door, spilling coffee all over my shirt.

As I walked into the house, disarray overwhelmed me. *Where to start?* I let out a grumpy sigh and trudged over to the kitchen sink. As I began washing the dishes, I realized how tense I was. My arms hurt from scrubbing so hard and fast. The dishes were getting *really* clean.

My mind wandered from reliving my irritations from the morning to the long list of the day's tasks hanging over me. With each distraction, my mood slumped lower. Then determination rose up in me. I was not going to struggle through the rest of my day that way. So I did the opposite of what I felt like doing. I chose joy and began to sing. One of my favorite church hymns came to mind:

I come to the garden alone
While the dew is still on the roses
And the voice I hear, falling on my ear,
the son of God discloses.
And He walks with me, and He talks with me,
And He tells me I am His own,
And the joy we share as we tarry there,
None other has ever known.

My spirit lightened and lifted. Suddenly, washing dishes became one of the most joyful things I had ever done! Time froze, and heaven touched earth as I met with Jesus in the enchanting garden of my soul.

We can easily become so busy and focused on caring for our children and completing our daily tasks that we feel like we have no time to do the things we enjoy or to spend time with God. Our minds and energy are pulled in a hundred directions, making it difficult to fully live in the present moment. As a result, our bodies and minds remain stuck in stress.

So how do we get unstuck and decompress? By adding back in those activities that we enjoy. If we are filling our days with work, chores, and caring for others, and we are not intentionally nurturing joy, it can be difficult to thrive. Reintroducing a personal interest or hobby for even ten minutes a day can help reduce stress and increase our enjoyment of life.

Yet deep and lasting joy is only found in the presence of God. When we practice Christian mindfulness, we immerse ourselves in the present moment while remaining aware of Jesus with us. This opens our hearts for him to fill us with abounding joy and peace. Our moods lift, our anxiety lightens, and he carries us above our stress. As Henri Nouwen wrote, "Joy does not simply happen to us. We have to choose joy and keep choosing it every day." But no one and nothing can ever steal your joy in the Lord.

When it's hard to find anything to be joyful about in your current circumstances, where can you find joy? In God's presence. In worshipping and loving him. In taking note of his many gifts and blessings on this very day. John Ortberg wrote, "If we don't rejoice today, we will not rejoice at all. If we wait until conditions are perfect, we will still be waiting when we die. If we are going to rejoice, it must be in *this* day."

Remember, Jesus is there with you in the most mundane minutes of your day. He wants you to live in his presence and talk with him even during unexciting and unpleasant activities like sitting at work, cooking dinner, and even changing diapers.

Discover joy in your present moment. When no beauty is blooming in your life, grow it. Plant what brings you delight—enjoy a hobby or use a gift or talent God has given you to help others. Meet Jesus in the garden of your soul and breathe in the sweet aroma of his presence. Sing until your heart sways to the harmony of your spirits communing. Tarry there with him and flourish in the joy of his presence.

Pray

Jesus, when I'm in your presence, you fill me with absolute joy, even amid my problems and pain. I worship you, and I long to know you more.

Ponder 2 MINUTES

Take a few minutes to record your thoughts.

1. What types of activities bring you joy? How can you include one in your week?

---

2. What's one way you can experience joy in God's presence throughout your day?

Practice 5 MINUTES

Delight in joyful communion with God.

Optional: Play a quiet worship song.

1. Begin by taking two slow, deep breaths.
2. Look inward and meet Jesus in the garden of your soul. Walk together through the lush floral pathway of the vibrant parts of your life as well as the overgrown and withering areas.
3. What does your garden look like? Where do you see joy blooming?

4. What would you like to "plant" to make your life more beautiful?

5. Simply be with Jesus, worship him, and together grow heavenly joy.

Plan

Practice God's presence throughout your day.

1. Set an hourly alarm to remind you to pause.

2. Take a deep breath and bring your awareness back to the present moment.

3. Whisper this prayer: "Jesus, I worship you. You fill me with extravagant joy."

4. Listen to a Christian radio station, sing a worship song, or recite a psalm from the Bible such as Psalm 95, 100, or 150.

REMEMBER

Grow joy in God's presence.

DAY 25

Connect with Others

Share each other's burdens, and in this way obey the law of Christ.

—Galatians 6:2

Shortly after moving back to the Nashville area, we began our search for a new church home. We visited several—well, *numerous*—congregations. We made valiant efforts to join a church community where our family felt welcomed and where attending was practical with Bethany Grace's physical and developmental disabilities. One church had twenty steps up to the kids' rooms with no elevator, and another offered earplugs because the service was so loud. We ended up attending one church every week for a year and signed up to join a small group Bible study, but the church never found a group for us to join, and we felt alone on Sunday mornings.

Then another special needs mom from Bethany Grace's preschool told me about a church near us that had a heart for families with disabilities. The church even offered a support group for parent caregivers. We mustered up the courage and walked into the small, packed room. As we joined the circle of chairs, warm smiles greeted us. The leader presented a short devotional, opened in prayer, then invited parents to share.

As I listened to the other parents tell their stories from the week and talk about their joys and challenges, I was surprised by how our own struggles were similar to the problems they were experiencing with their children, families, and faith. I sat up and intently listened as one father shared about the battles they were having with their son's school. Then a mother shared about her heartbreaking consultation with her daughter's doctor. I watched as other caregivers listened empathically and offered words of encouragement to one another. Todd and I had found what we had been missing terribly—connection and mutual support with other parents in a Christian community and a safe place where we could belong and grow.

We're not psychologically or spiritually designed to walk this trying parenting journey alone. We need friendships with other parents and fellowship with other Christians. Unfortunately, stress can draw us into ourselves and away from God and other people. But God created us to depend on others to encourage us, speak into our struggles, and guide us closer to Jesus. And God also desires for us to uplift and help others with the same comfort he gives us (see 2 Corinthians 1:4).

In stressful parenting situations, quality social support can greatly improve our mental well-being and reduce burnout. Life is better when we have other parents we can talk to and spend time with through meals, having fun, and sharing advice. Especially if your child is experiencing a particular problem, I encourage you to join a support group of other parents navigating similar issues.

A proven aspect of lowering stress and coping with parenting demands is engaging in a supportive faith community. We grow spiritually in unique ways when we're in fellowship with others. God designed us to draw closer to him by sharing life with other Christians. Other believers can guide us in seeing our lives from God's perspective and help us reframe our way of thinking about our problems. Larry Crabb wrote, "Spiritual togetherness, what I call *connecting,* creates movement: *Togetherness* in Christ encourages *movement* toward Christ." In community with other families, Todd and I have grown spiritually, deepened our marriage relationship, and strengthened our parenting skills.

God created us to need relationships. He loves us and speaks to us through fellow Christians, and he wants us to love him by uplifting others in their struggles. Reaching out and being vulnerable with others takes energy and courage. But Jesus reaches out to you through others, and he will bless you through your relationships and the way you share life in Christian community. So live life in connection with others and draw closer to Jesus in the process.

Pray

Lord Jesus, help me move closer to you through rich relationships with others. Please bring me a good friend and guide me to a loving Christian community in which I can grow.

Ponder 2 MINUTES

Take a few minutes to record your thoughts.

1. Name some meaningful connections you have or long to have in Christian community or with other parents.

---

2. What's one way you can grow a friendship or become more engaged in a church?

Practice 3 MINUTES

Ask God for community.

1. Begin by taking two slow, deep breaths.
2. Meditate on 2 Corinthians 1:4 for a moment:

   "He comforts us in all our troubles so that we can comfort others. When they are troubled, we will be able to give them the same comfort God has given us."

3. Close your eyes and picture a person with whom you might develop a stronger relationship.

4. If no one comes to mind, ask Jesus to show you someone.

5. Briefly pray for that person.

Plan

Deepen a connection.

1. Reach out to one other parent today.

2. Plan a time to meet for coffee, share a meal, go for a walk, or talk in some other way.

REMEMBER

Live life in connection with others.

Part 6

Releasing Painful Emotions

DAY 26

Explore Your Emotions

You have searched me, LORD,
and you know me.
—Psalm 139:1, NIV

We fought our way up the gym bleachers and squeezed into the sixth row. I searched for Bethany Grace among the mass of eighth graders. She was graduating middle school after doctors had told us she wouldn't survive to her first birthday.

I spotted her in the navy dress within a sea of white. I scanned the other rows. Almost all the girls were wearing white. I didn't have parent friends outside Bethany Grace's special education class, so I hadn't heard about the tradition.

The other students were all chatting and laughing. Bethany Grace looked scared and excited at the same time. Painful mixed emotions rose up in me. I pushed my feelings down during the ceremony. Then it came time to award the diplomas.

Bethany Grace's row stood and lined up. I sat on the edge of my seat, phone ready to record.

"Bethany Grace Evans." The principal beamed as my beautiful and inspiring daughter sprang across the stage and hugged him.

"A-w-e." The crowd stood, loudly clapping and cheering.

My daughter proudly showed off her diploma as she paraded past the other students and parents. Tears of joy, gratitude, grief, and pride welled up in my eyes. This time, I let them flow.

We sometimes ignore our emotions or tell ourselves we shouldn't be feeling a certain way. We may not have the time to deal with a surge of anger or a wave of sadness, so we push our feelings back down. But when we deny our painful emotions, they only grow in power and can take over our mental and emotional well-being. The pressure continues to build until we either erupt on someone else or turn on ourselves.

Emotions are complex, and we experience them as a whole self, meaning we are connected to our emotions throughout our body and mind. We can lower our stress and the intensity of our emotions by simply listening to what our feelings are trying to tell us. A healthy way to process our emotions is to mindfully observe them. This means experiencing our emotions in the present moment without judging them, trying to prevent or block them, distracting ourselves from them, or holding on to them.

When you notice yourself experiencing a negative emotion, step back from it and be an objective observer. Identify the emotion (e.g., anger, sadness, fear). Then see if you can narrow it down further. For example, first label it "sad," then see if you can describe it more specifically as "disappointed," "discouraged," "lonely," or "heartbroken." Next, acknowledge that you're feeling that way: "I'm feeling disappointed." This simple practice of naming your emotions can help you better manage them. Putting feelings into words, whether by writing them down or saying them out loud, calms the amygdala (the emotionally reactive part of the brain); lowers stress, anxiety, and fear; and can improve your mental and physical health.

Another way to help manage your emotions is to be self-compassionate and curious about why you might be feeling a particular emotion. Alicia Michelle encourages us to "see painful emotions as compassionate invitations to slow down and ask ourselves what's going on. Emotions should be viewed not as an enemy to fight but a curiosity to consider." So when you feel a certain way, take a moment and reflect. Even if you can't pinpoint a specific event, consider all you've been through that could prompt that emotion. Maybe it's even a thought. What do you think this emotion and your reaction are trying to tell you?

The One who knows you best is there with you in this process. Jesus understands what you're experiencing and why. He knows you intimately and knows precisely what you need. Your emotions are spiritual, from deep within your soul, not just from your mind and body. Explore your emotions with Jesus through the help of the Holy Spirit. Allow yourself to feel your emotions in his presence. Look at scriptures about those emotions and listen for the Spirit's guidance in how to move forward. Then stay in tune with your emotions and pray about them throughout the day.

Pray

Jesus, you know me because you have seen deep into my heart. Help me discover the source of my painful emotions and process them with you.

Ponder 2 MINUTES

Take a few minutes to record your thoughts.

1. Name any hard emotions that have come up for you lately.

---

2. Brainstorm possible causes of these emotions.

Practice 5 MINUTES

Check in with your body.

1. Begin by taking two slow, deep breaths.
2. Sit comfortably in your chair or lie flat on your bed or on the floor.
3. Simply be present in your body, mind, and spirit. Become aware of God's presence with you.
4. Beginning with your toes, scan your body, pausing at

each muscle group to notice how you're feeling in that part of your body. Observe any discomfort, pain, relaxation, or tension.

5. Welcome with curiosity any emotions that surface. Name the emotions. You can pray:

"Jesus, I'm feeling ____________________."

6. Continue scanning your body to the top of your head and end with two slow, deep breaths.

Plan

Observe your emotions.

When you experience a hard emotion today:

1. Pause and notice where you're feeling the emotion in your body.
2. Name the emotion.
3. Be curious about what's causing the emotion.
4. Share your feelings with Jesus.

REMEMBER

Explore your emotions with Jesus.

DAY 27

Reframe Your Perspective

Do not conform to the pattern of this world, but be transformed by the renewing of your mind.

—Romans 12:2, NIV

We hiked up the street from the pier in the chilly coastal drizzle. A line had already formed outside the small fish restaurant. An employee opened the door, and the crowd crammed into the small room. The aroma of freshly caught haddock frying wafted toward me as we entered.

"Can you order while I try to stake out some tables?" Todd asked me across the noise of the crowd.

"How many meals should I order?"

"Seven." He disappeared with the kids through the old Western-style swinging doors.

I surveyed the baskets of fish in the display case, then looked up at the simple menu. "One piece plus chips—$18. Two pieces plus chips—$24."

Wait, did Todd mean one piece or two pieces? Oh dear.

I recalled the famished look on his face. I was afraid I would get too little and he would still be hungry.

The two-piece meal seems like a better deal. I'm sure he meant two pieces.

I reached the register. "I'd like seven two-piece meals, please."

"Are you sure? How many of you are there?"

"There's seven of us. Yes."

The restless crowd behind me stared as the mountain of fish grew on the counter. When the server brought the trays, Todd gawked. "How much did you order? How are we going to eat all this?"

"You said seven meals," I shot back in defense.

"Not two-piece meals! The pieces are huge."

I stared at triple the amount of fish I imagined it would be. We definitely enjoyed the freshest fried fish we'd ever tasted, but even after giving two meals away, we still ate enough for a lifetime.

Our thoughts influence our mood and behaviors. How we look at ourselves, our circumstances, our children, and others can produce either increased stress and negative emotions or a hopeful outlook and a grateful attitude. We all approach life and parenting through a lens of some inaccurate beliefs and unhelpful ways of thinking called cognitive distortions. Some examples of these unhealthy thinking patterns include:

- making assumptions or jumping to conclusions
- all-or-nothing and black-and-white thinking
- using "should" or "must" and "always" or "never" statements
- magnifying the negative or minimizing the situation
- overpersonalizing

When we look through these filters, we can't clearly see the facts. By removing the cognitive distortion, we can reframe our thoughts to be more accurate statements about ourselves, the situation, our children, and others. We can respond to our children with greater insight and openness and address them more effectively.

Emotional distortion is another unhealthy way we can come to conclusions. It is a one-sided perspective where we believe something must be true because it's how we feel. Joyce Meyer taught, "We need to be able to step back from our situations and see them from God's perspective. Then we need to make decisions based on what we *know* rather than on what we *feel.*"

What we believe about ourselves and others shapes our thoughts. To see ourselves and our lives as clearly as God does, we need to adjust our lens, focus our attention on Jesus, and filter our thoughts through Scripture. In Christian mindfulness, we learn to observe our thoughts and seek God's thoughts, because our thoughts are always imperfect. To reframe our thoughts, we must first become aware of them. We must be open to the work of delving in and examining our beliefs with the help of the Holy Spirit, Scripture, and others in the Christian community.

Ultimately, God does the work of transforming us. Only he can help us change the way we think by replacing our distorted beliefs with more accurate ones in line with his Word. The renewal of our minds is a continual process. As we meditate on the new and truer thoughts, our neural pathways will be reconstructed and our souls transformed.

When you gain a clearer picture of your true identity and worth in Jesus, you will see yourself and your life from a new perspective. Breathe in God's transformative Spirit of truth and love and release your old way of thinking.

Pray

Jesus, reveal to me the ways I'm not seeing clearly. Help me look through the lens of your perspective and reframe my thoughts to reflect your truth. Transform me and renew my mind.

Ponder 2 MINUTES

Take a few minutes to record your thoughts.

1. Look back at the different types of distorted thinking patterns on page 152. List any you experience in your parenting and daily life.

2. Name any thoughts or beliefs that may not be entirely accurate, healthy, or based in Scripture.

Practice 4 MINUTES

Mindfully observe your thoughts.

1. Begin by taking two slow, deep breaths.

   As you inhale, pray: "Transform my thoughts."

   As you exhale, pray: "Renew my mind."

2. Still your body and allow your thoughts to come as they please.

3. For a couple of minutes, simply observe any thoughts that arise.

4. If there are any thoughts that unsettle you, pray about them. Ask the Holy Spirit to reframe your beliefs to match his truth.

Plan

Reframe your thoughts.

1. As you go about your day, observe your thoughts any time you're feeling an emotion.

2. Identify any unhelpful thinking patterns through which you might be filtering your beliefs.

3. Ask Jesus to help you reframe your thoughts to match his.

4. Consider looking up Scripture passages that speak to the issue.

REMEMBER

Reframe your perspective with God's truth.

DAY 28

Cure Envy with Empathy

It's healthy to be content,
but envy can eat you up.
—Proverbs 14:30, CEV

"Can you and Bethany Grace come over for a playdate?" My friend's cheerfulness punched me in my gut.

I gazed over at my medically fragile infant lying in her medical crib. The sounds of oxygen flowing, the feeding pump turning, and the heart monitors beeping reminded me of my reality. Tubes and wires tethered Bethany Grace to her bed. *No, she can't come over for a play-date! Why can't my friends understand?*

I tried to will the tears back into my eyes. "No, she's only allowed to leave the house to go for doctors' appointments, and we can't have anyone over because of germs." I furrowed my brows.

My friend and I had shared similar due dates. She had enjoyed a huge baby bump and a seamless pregnancy. My pregnancy had been a nightmare, and Bethany Grace had arrived over two months early. *Her baby and other children are all healthy and typically developing.* I longed for that so badly. Envy for her joy burned in my chest.

"Oh, okay. Maybe next time."

As I put down my phone, I imagined her calling one of our other friends and the two of them sitting on a blanket while drinking coffee and helping their babies practice tummy time.

I'm never going to have a normal life like other moms. It's not fair. I want what they have.

I lost the battle with my tears the rest of the day.

Envy turns poisonous. Yes, I was processing intense grief and trying to manage inconceivable stress. But my desire to have the blessings of other moms was eating me alive, breeding increased suffering and grimmer depression. I didn't have the capacity to be happy for others or to have empathy for their struggles.

As parents, we have hopes and dreams for our families, our children's futures, and possibly our careers. It can be tempting to compare our circumstances to the situations and successes of other parents and families. However, assuming those families enjoy life more, believing they have it easier, or wishing for what they have can add stress and foster a negative focus and attitude. Coveting what we don't have can make us sick mentally, emotionally, spiritually, and even physically. Envy grows like a cancer and can cause depression, anger, anxiety, shame, guilt, resentment, and interpersonal conflict. It stems from a complex mix of primary emotions lying deep inside us, including anger, sadness, and fear.

To cure envy, we have to cut out the tumor of discontentment. How do we do that? We give Jesus, the Great Physician, the scalpel. Spending time in prayer acknowledging our feelings, reflecting on what might be causing them, and processing the deeper emotions with Jesus will weaken the grip of envy. Charles H. Spurgeon taught, "The cure for envy lies in living under a constant sense of the divine presence, worshiping God and communing with Him all day long, however long the day may seem."

When we bring our struggles with envy to God, he restores our hearts by filling us with true contentment in him. But we also have to intentionally cultivate a content heart.

Working toward acceptance, thanking God, and choosing joy will heal the illness of envy and free us to thrive in the blessings God has given us. Because love does not envy (1 Corinthians 13:4), envy cannot survive in a healthy heart that beats with gratitude to God and with love for others. Showing kindness and empathy to others for the ways their families are struggling will protect our own hearts from envy.

God's plan for your life and your child(ren) and his purposes for what's best for your family have nothing to do with how other families are living. Discover your own blessings and embrace your family's unique gifts and needs. Consent to God to perform surgery on your heart to repair the damage from envy. And then may he fill you with deep contentment and joy, love, and empathy for others.

Pray

Jesus, my Healer, open my heart and reveal any feelings of anger, bitterness, envy, sadness, resentment, or fear. Remove my toxic thoughts and fill that space with love for you and others.

Ponder 2 MINUTES

Take a few minutes to record your thoughts.

1. Name a way you're envious of another parent or family.

2. How can you be genuinely happy for them or show empathy in their struggles?

Practice 5 MINUTES

Remove envy from your heart.

1. Begin by taking two slow, deep breaths.
2. Place a hand on your heart. Focus on Jesus as the center of your being.
3. Close your eyes and picture that other person's life.
4. Allow your thoughts and emotions to surface.
5. As envy, anger, sadness, fear, or other painful feelings arise, pray:

Jesus, please heal my heart and fill me with gratitude and contentment.

Plan

Express love and empathy.

Think of something nice you can do for another person or family and take a step in saying or doing something kind for them. Some ideas might include:

1. Send an encouraging message or call them.
2. Drop off a plate of cookies.
3. Offer to pick up or watch their child.
4. Invite them over for a playdate or a meal.

REMEMBER

Cure envy by showing love and empathy.

DAY 29

Uncover Anger

Don't sin by letting anger control you.
Think about it overnight and remain silent.
—Psalm 4:4

Yellow. I punched the accelerator and checked my rearview mirror as the traffic light switched to red. I looked back at the road just in time to see a car cut me off, nearly clipping the front of my van. I slammed on the brakes. My nostrils flared, and my jaw tensed like I was preparing to charge into battle. I restrained myself from honking.

I can't believe he just did that! My face reddened, and choice words threatened to come out of my mouth. I realized my aggravated hands were gripping the steering wheel. I peeked at my daughter in the back seat. Then I took a slow, deep breath and exhaled my hot annoyance. My arms relaxed, and my face softened. With my temper now quieted, I was able to hear my thoughts. *Why did I react so strongly?*

By that point, I was thinking out loud. Hopefully, the drivers around me just assumed I was talking on my car's speakerphone.

"For starters, I'm exhausted. And we should have left the house sooner. We're going to be late."

Now I was curious and more willing to be honest. "I feel bad about running late to Bethany Grace's doctor appointment. I'm going to be embarrassed."

And there it was—the real root of my thorny attitude: my feelings of guilt. That weed of shame was squeezing the joy out of my day.

Everyone experiences anger at times for different reasons. The pressure builds as we try to balance too many responsibilities, work demands, relationship issues, unresolved emotional experiences, and our children's needs and possibly behavioral problems. Exhaustion from parenting can easily lead to burnout, which often results in angry outbursts. Uncontrolled anger can cause any number of health problems for parents. This tension can also create distance and resentment in our relationships with our children and result in serious negative health and developmental outcomes for them.

You may feel like you don't get angry. But anger can take many forms and look like various emotions. For some people, managing anger is an obvious struggle. Some parents become frustrated, yell, or even become abusive. For others, the symptoms of anger are not so apparent. They may turn their rage inward by doling out self-criticism, shutting down, or becoming avoidant.

But the outcomes of anger should not be ignored. Anger causes physiological changes, including increased heart rate and blood pressure, adrenaline production, and muscle tension. We can also experience cognitive effects such as inattention and difficulty making decisions.

To parent calmly, we can use the coping skills we've been learning, including practicing mindfulness and progressive muscle relaxation. Deep, abdominal breathing is one of the most effective ways to reduce our stress reactions. Breathing exercises help reverse the physical responses of anger and give us time to reflect, think more rationally, and respond more effectively. By pausing and breathing, we can reduce the intensity of our anger reaction and treat ourselves and others with kindness in our words and actions.

But anger is typically a secondary emotion, meaning a more intense primary emotion lies beneath the surface. We express anger to protect ourselves from dealing with the painful emotions that are really driving our reactions. Primary emotions can include feelings of disappointment, inadequacy, resentment, pride, embarrassment, fear, sadness, guilt, or shame. This quote often attributed to C. S. Lewis beautifully captures the nature of this complex emotion: "I sat with my anger long enough until she told me her real name was grief."

To resolve anger and lower the intensity of our negative emotions, we must identify and address the underlying feelings and core beliefs about ourselves and others. This process takes time. And sometimes only professional counseling can help us process our hurts.

However you process your anger, remember to take this reaction first and foremost to God. When you pause to breathe and recenter your mind on Jesus, you open a space in your soul to meet with the

Holy Spirit. He can show you the parts of your heart where anger grows, and he will take you to the places in your soul where anger first took root. Go deeper with your loving and supportive Counselor and Healer to uncover the true source of your anger and deal with it. With God's help, take control of your anger and root it out.

Pray

Holy Spirit, please meet me here. I'm willing to dig deeper to uncover the root of my anger. Help me deal with these emotions and heal.

Ponder 3 MINUTES

Take a few minutes to record your thoughts.

1. Name a situation that makes you feel angry.

2. How does your irritation typically manifest, whether internally or externally?

3. What emotions might lie beneath the surface of your anger?

Practice 5 MINUTES

Uncover the root of your anger.

1. Begin by taking two slow, deep breaths.
2. Sit in silence and open a space in your soul to meet with the Holy Spirit.
3. Picture that situation that irritates you. What thoughts come up? How do you feel inside your body?
4. Ask the Holy Spirit to take you below the surface and show you the root of your anger.
5. Pray: "Help me heal this hurt and replace anger with love."

Plan

Reflect on your reactions.

1. When you find yourself becoming frustrated today, pause.
2. Take two deep breaths.
3. Ask God to help you see what is really causing you to be upset.
4. Respond to yourself and others in love.

REMEMBER

Address the root of your anger.

DAY 30

Release Your Fears

I prayed to the LORD, and he answered me.
He freed me from all my fears.

—Psalm 34:4

Homecoming Day finally arrived. Balloons greeted us as we carried our fragile daughter, Bethany Grace, into the house. The neonatal intensive care unit had been her only home for three months. My face beamed in joy and pride.

But within twenty-four hours I began to experience levels of apprehension I didn't know were possible. Medical machines beeped and alarms sounded night and day. I lay awake with my eyes fixed on her heart rate number, just waiting for her pulse to climb too high and her oxygen level to drop too low. Dread paralyzed my body. Anticipation of the next 911 call stole my sleep. The more I focused on my fears, the more they consumed me. I grabbed on to them, and they yanked my mind into the future. I thought if I could somehow worry enough, I could prevent my worst nightmares from coming true.

But I couldn't free my mind from my fears on my own. It was when I sought the Lord and focused my heart and mind on him that he pulled me out of my distress. It was three years after my daughter came home from the hospital when I cried out to God and released my fears to him, one at a time. There on the edge of a gently flowing stream, he lifted the weighty drape of dread off my shoulders and steadied my shaking hands.

Though many of my fears were extreme, they were mostly based in reality. Bethany Grace did often go into medical crises. But traumatic events such as the ones our family went through can keep our brains and bodies trapped in a hypervigilant loop. As a result, many of my fears became overexaggerated, and my fixation on potential future bad events amplified my anxiety.

Living with fears of the future keeps our body's stress response system activated and exacerbates anxiety. Some of our fears are based in reality—we may be facing a real and present threat to our family's well-being or to ourselves. Yet many of our fears about our children are never going to come true. And many times, our fears grow out of proportion to the actual facts of the situation the more we dwell on them. We could lessen most of our apprehension if we would only surrender it to God and use some simple coping strategies. However, situations that involve resolving trauma may require professional treatment.

When we try to stop thinking about the situations that cause us stress, we actually give more power to our fears. The more we attempt to silence our anxious thoughts, the louder they become. An effective way to quiet our fears is to avoid struggling with our anxious thoughts and instead gently return our focus to our breath and the present moment. Even as you practice being mindful, you can expect your mind to wander back to your anxious thoughts. That's okay. Simply continue to redirect your mind back to the present moment. This takes practice, but you can develop the habit. Celebrate those moments as you hone this skill!

When we refocus our minds on the holy presence of Jesus, he can draw our attention back to depending on his Spirit for help and peace. Fear loses its power. Jackie Smith-Bell reminds us that "when we focus on God, we invite His peace into our fear." So call on the name of Jesus, and he will answer you and rescue you from all your fears. Release each one into his open hands.

Pray

Jesus, I cry out to you. Rescue me from my fears. Bring me back to centering my mind on breathing in your peace.

Ponder 2 MINUTES

Take a few minutes to record your thoughts.

1. What are some of your fears?

2. How might those fears be affecting you?

Practice 5 MINUTES

Release your fears.

1. Begin by taking two slow, deep breaths.
2. Close your eyes and picture yourself sitting with Jesus by a brook under a canopy of autumn leaves that are lazily floating to the ground.
3. Notice your thoughts and emotions. As a specific fear comes to mind, pick up a leaf and name it.
4. Hand the leaf to Jesus and pray, "Lord Jesus, free me from my fear."
5. Watch as Jesus releases your fear in the flowing stream and it drifts out of sight.
6. Each time a fear comes to mind, repeat steps 3 through 5.

Plan

Release two more fears today.

1. When you feel anxiety or fear, picture yourself there in those autumn woods.
2. Pick up a leaf and label it what you fear most.

3. Give your fear to Jesus and watch as it floats out of sight.

REMEMBER

Release your fears in the stream of God's Spirit.

Part 7

Receiving God's Power

DAY 31

Welcome Freedom from Guilt

Even if we feel guilty, God is greater than our feelings, and he knows everything.

—1 John 3:20

I looked at my watch as I trekked up the hill. *I shouldn't still be here.*

I popped into each house and checked on the new patients. Before heading home, I stepped outside and, noticing the path to the river, decided to hike down for just a minute. With the recent heavy rain, the current was flowing high on the rocks. Like the muddy water, my murky thoughts were clouded with self-blame.

I've been neglecting Todd and the kids. I'm out of touch with what's going on at their schools. I've been a better therapist than a wife and mom.

I turned to jog down to my car. After driving the fifty minutes home, I took a deep breath and opened the back door.

"Hi, honey. How was your day?" Todd had dinner waiting for me.

I dropped my work bag into a chair. "I'm exhausted."

"It seems like your job's taking a lot out of you." He set my plate down in front of me.

"Things are really stressful here too. I've let a lot go. I've barely spent time with you all, and you've been picking up the slack with all the housework." I took a bite of the savory burrito.

"You're working because we need the income, remember? You shouldn't feel bad. You're doing the best you can." His deep brown eyes were filled with sincerity.

Maybe I *was* doing the best I could, and the guilt I was feeling wasn't warranted.

Many parents wade through high levels of guilt. We may feel guilty for being away at work, not spending more time with our children, taking time for ourselves, or not helping our own parents. We might shame ourselves for past decisions we wish we could change or blame ourselves for our children's struggles. These feelings of guilt emerge from believing we've not measured up to other parents, societal pressures, or our own expectations.

The feeling of guilt is functional. We feel guilty when we believe we've done something wrong. But there's *justified guilt,* and then there's *unjustified guilt.* Justified guilt is when we've gone against our faith beliefs, morals, or values. Guilt prompts us to confess to God, receive forgiveness, forgive ourselves, and correct the wrong. In contrast, guilt is unjustified when we have done nothing that goes against our beliefs, morals, or values.

Condemning ourselves with unjustified guilt does not serve us in any way. Unjustified guilt grows out of negative self-talk and self-blame. To improve our psychological health, we can replace this undeserved self-criticism with self-compassion. Simply put, extending ourselves forgiveness and compassion will reduce our parenting stress and make us more compassionate parents. To be self-compassionate, we must first be mindful of the situation and name the facts. Then we can determine a more objective and accurate statement about ourselves.

To do this, we need to cultivate a good relationship with God, since what we believe about God shapes how we treat ourselves. If we feel that God is unapproachable and we avoid sharing our emotions with him, then we are less likely to respond to our shortcomings with gentleness and understanding. But when we have confidence in our relationship with a loving God and trust that he is good, we can grant ourselves grace. As Kristin J. Homan wrote, "Those who perceive God as compassionate are able to extend compassion to themselves."

Our self-condemning hearts muddle our thoughts, emotions, and connection with God and others. We can't remedy our guilt on our own. We need God's help to determine if our guilt is justified or unjustified. If it's not justified, we can work with him to see our situations and ourselves clearer, reframe our thoughts, and extend ourselves compassion. If our guilt is justified, we can confess our sins to God and receive his forgiveness. If we then continue to chastise ourselves, that voice is not from God.

God is intimately aware of your feelings of guilt and your contrite heart. He sees your emotional pain through eyes of compassion and love. Let him free you from the sludge of self-condemnation that drags down your heart. Follow him to the clear, bottomless pool of his mercy and grace.

Pray

Jesus, help me clearly see the source of my self-blame. Please free me from my condemning heart and heavy guilt so I can live joyfully.

Ponder 2 MINUTES

Take a few minutes to record your thoughts.

1. What are some situations you feel guilty about?

2. Name any feelings of guilt that might be unjustified.

Practice 5 MINUTES

Release unjustified guilt.

1. Begin by taking two slow, deep breaths.
2. Select one of the situations that is causing you feelings of unjustified guilt.
3. Pray: "Jesus, free me from my self-blame and guilt."
4. Begin tapping the top of your legs gently and slowly.

Alternate between tapping your right leg and left leg at a steady pace. Breathe deeply and slowly.

5. Continue tapping and repeating the prayer until the intensity of your tension and negative emotions lowers.

Plan

Check the facts.

1. When you find yourself feeling guilty or blaming yourself, pray about your feelings. With God's help, determine if your guilt is justified or unjustified.

2. If justified: Confess your sin to God, accept his forgiveness, forgive yourself, and right the wrong.

3. If unjustified: Reframe your self-talk to a more accurate and self-compassionate statement. Practice the bilateral leg-tapping exercise.

REMEMBER

Let God free you from the mire of guilt.

DAY 32

Experience Indescribable Peace

Don't worry about anything; instead, pray about everything. Tell God what you need, and thank him for all he has done. Then you will experience God's peace, which exceeds anything we can understand.

—Philippians 4:6–7

Major life changes lay just ahead as we prepared to move four hours across the state of Tennessee. The pieces seemed to be coming together, but there were so many pieces.

Todd and I were feverishly handling all the details of relocating our complex family. While closing out his seven years as a youth pastor, he labored to lock in his graduate school position, finish renovations on the new house, and plan for substantial financial shifts. I worked to transfer the kids' schools, Bethany Grace's home health nursing, her team of doctors and specialists, and developmental therapies.

"How do you look so peaceful?" My friend lovingly bubble-wrapped one of my knickknacks.

I sighed. "I don't know. This *is* one of the most stressful times of my life. I can't explain it."

As I spoke, her eyes got big and her brows raised. She shrugged. "I would be so stressed out if I were going through this."

"I *am* very stressed, but I just keep praying, and God keeps helping me." I gazed upward.

Everything did fall into place after months of intense work. God provided all we needed and more.

It would be surprising if, as parents working tirelessly to care for our families during these uncertain times, we weren't a little stressed. It would seem odd if we walked around with our minds totally at peace about our children's safety, social media use, futures, and mental, emotional, and spiritual development.

All of us worry at times, if not daily, and achieving peace of mind can feel impossible. Eight in ten parents report they "often" or "very often" worry about at least one aspect of their child's life. A miniscule 2 percent of parents "rarely" or "never" worry about their child. Forty percent of U.S. parents are extremely or very concerned about the future of their child's mental health, and 35 percent worry about their child being bullied.

As we know, when we constantly worry about providing for our families' needs and protecting our children, anxiety and mental and physical tension intensify. And the more we worry, the more our kids worry and develop anxiety. I hope you've experienced how focusing on one issue and one moment at a time can relax your mind and body and how regularly practicing mindfulness can reduce your stress and improve your children's psychological well-being.

Yet true peace comes from praying often and recentering our minds on God's presence in our lives. When we continually return to the presence of Jesus and pray about our worries, he protects our hearts and minds from the damage that stress and anxiety can do to us mentally and spiritually (see Philippians 4:7). It *is* possible for us to shift our focus to the assurance of God's care and provision. Peace is something we can actually experience and is what he wants for us despite our uncertainties and fears. In fact, it is through calling out to God in our anxious struggles that we can truly experience unexplainable peace. Elisabeth Elliot wrote, "The secret is *Christ* in *me,* not me in a different set of circumstances." Regardless of what's happening in our lives, God can help us lay our heads down at night and sleep in peace (see Psalm 4:8).

God understands your parenting struggles and fears. He invites you to ask him for what you need, thank him for all he is doing, and receive his transcendent peace. Then you will grow closer to him in trust, gratitude, and hope. He will quiet your mind and body and draw you into inner tranquility. Pray about everything and experience God's indescribable peace.

Pray

Jesus, true peace is found in trusting you. Protect my mind and health from the toxic effects of stress and worry. Thank you for all you have done in my life and for my family.

Ponder 2 MINUTES

Take a few minutes to record your thoughts.

1. When you think about your family's well-being, what thoughts keep you from experiencing peace of mind?

2. What worries could you pray about more often?

Practice 4 MINUTES

Experience God's peace.

1. Begin by taking two slow, deep breaths.
2. Sit in the present moment with your stress, noticing how you feel in your mind and body.
3. As a worry comes to mind, name it. Then pray:

   God, please help me with ________________.

4. Take deep breaths:

   Inhale: *Thank you, Lord*

   Exhale: *for your peace.*

5. Repeat step 3 and 4 until your mind and body feel more relaxed.

Plan

Write down your worries and requests.

1. When you notice yourself feeling anxious, pause and note your worries either electronically or in a notebook.

2. Talk to God about your concerns, thank him for all he has done, trust him to act, and then receive his incomprehensible peace.

REMEMBER

Ask God for what you need, trust him, and experience his indescribable peace.

DAY 33

Receive His Grace

God saved you by his grace when you believed. And you can't take credit for this; it is a gift from God.

—Ephesians 2:8

Bethany Grace proudly held her race shirt and bib number as we headed over to the adaptive bike station. The volunteer helped her climb onto the shiny red trike she would be borrowing for the triathlon. As the volunteer adjusted the seat, side supports, and straps, the physical therapist who had recently reevaluated Bethany Grace walked over. She was the one who had told us about this race for children with disabilities.

Cheer filled her voice. "How does she like the trike?"

"Oh, she's in heaven." I gazed at my giddy daughter.

"Good. How big is your vehicle?"

"We . . . came in our van . . . ?"

"Great. Because you're taking this trike home." Delight filled her eyes.

Tears began streaming down my shocked face. *This is too much. We can't accept this. We can't repay the company.* Then a sense of humility and immense gratitude washed over me.

I hugged her. "Thank you. This is such an amazing gift."

"You're welcome. It's my pleasure to help. I hope she enjoys many hours of riding."

Our therapist had advocated with several organizations to get this very expensive, specialized bike donated to Bethany Grace with all the exact specs she needed. We hadn't earned this astounding gift, and we couldn't have afforded to purchase one.

Joy beamed on our daughter's face as she pedaled past us. Her laughter was contagious and her zest for life inspired all those who cheered her on.

Many of us have difficulty accepting gifts, especially when they're expensive. We also tend to resist receiving grace, acts of kindness, assistance, and mercy from others. We can easily fall into a performance mentality, constantly striving to achieve success for ourselves and approval from others . . . or even from God. But striving to earn God's favor can create a never-ending battle of working to feel like we're good enough parents or Christians.

Our relationship with God can either calm our stress or cause us more stress depending on whether we accept or reject his grace. God's grace is his gift of unmerited favor and salvation. He takes pleasure in freely blessing us with abundant life and in having a relationship with us. Living in the freedom of his unconditional grace is how we ultimately cope with life's daily struggles, acknowledge our imperfections, and thrive in stronger mental health. Christians who better understand and appreciate grace are less anxious and depressed. Embracing God's grace also strengthens our relationships with others, including our children and spouses. When we accept God's grace, we are better able to extend grace and parent more patiently.

God's gift of grace and mercy is very costly, and it's something we could never pay for ourselves, no matter how hard we try for the rest of our lives. Our freedom comes from the jubilant truth and reprieve that we can never do enough to earn God's love nor do anything to lose his love. Oh, hallelujah! It's already completely finished! So we can stop trying. Through our faith in Jesus, we are instantly enough. We are made whole and already have his boundless love, remarkable grace, and priceless mercy.

Accepting God's grace is a prerequisite to flourishing. Jesus is offering his lavish love and glorious grace. We just have to be willing to open our hands to gratefully accept and enjoy his extravagant gift. Then he draws us closer to him and into an intimate and authentic relationship. "See what great love the Father has lavished on us, that we should be called children of God! And that is what we are!" (1 John 3:1, NIV)

Remember that you can rest securely in your unbreakable bond with God. He not only unconditionally accepts you, he delights in you. And just like your child will never understand how much you profoundly and unconditionally love them and would sacrifice for them, your heavenly Father, the Holy Spirit, and Jesus cherish you more than you could ever realize. Open your hands to Jesus and accept God's extravagant grace—the gift of never feeling like you have to earn his love ever again.

Pray

Jesus, unclench my hands and open my heart to receive your beautiful gift of grace. Teach me to live in the freedom of knowing I don't need to earn your love and acceptance.

Ponder 2 MINUTES

Take a few minutes to record your thoughts.

1. In what areas of your life do you feel like you have to do more to earn favor with God and others?

2. How would embracing God's grace in every aspect of your life free you to live more fully?

Practice 3 MINUTES

Accept God's grace.

1. Begin by taking two slow, deep breaths.

2. Place your hands on the center of your chest. Continue slow abdominal breathing.

3. After a minute, open your hands and hold them in front of you. Gaze upward.

4. Inhale: *Jesus, I accept*

Exhale: *your gift of grace.*

5. Rest here for a moment, offering this breath prayer.

Plan

Center your heart.

Pause two more times today:

1. Place your hands on the center of your chest.
2. Take slow, deep breaths.
3. Each time as you inhale, simply pray the word "grace."

REMEMBER

Open your hands to receive God's extravagant gift of grace.

DAY 34

Renew Your Strength

But those who trust in the LORD will find new strength.
They will soar high on wings like eagles.

—Isaiah 40:31

Pounding rain beat against the roof as Todd and I scrambled through the house with flashlights checking all the windows. We had just replaced the carpet. Our first showing was scheduled for the next morning. We needed to sell our home before moving from the Chicago suburbs back to Tennessee.

As we sprinted down the stairs to the finished basement, the sound of whooshing quickened our hearts. We panicked. Gushing water already filled the laundry area and was quickly approaching the carpet. When the storm knocked out the power, the sump pump had quit working too.

Todd, my mother, my mother-in-law, and I quickly formed a bucket relay. We filled our buckets, climbed the stairs, ducked out into the electrical storm to dump the water, and then repeated the whole process. We kept passing each other on the stairs as we desperately fought to hold back the flood. I struggled, still regaining my strength from giving birth to our first child just eight weeks earlier. I listened for the baby monitor and intermittently ran up to the nursery to nurse and change diapers before resuming the race.

As I climbed the steps, I prayed, "God, please don't let our house flood."

The longer the night went on, the more slowly I dragged. *God, help me keep going.*

Around three in the morning, the power finally came back on, and we collapsed into bed. As I drove to work a few hours later, I noticed many of our neighbors carrying carpet outside.

"Thank you, God, for helping us discover the flooding and for giving us the strength to endure."

We received a contract on our house that same day.

Most parents are drained. Fifty-seven percent of U.S. parents report they're burned out. Burnout occurs when the chronic stress overwhelms our ability to cope. When our stressors outweigh our available resources, we can become physically, mentally, and emotionally exhausted, as well as feel detached from our children. Parenting burnout can also lead to child behavioral and emotional problems.

Attempting to be self-sufficient and push through on our own can cause discouragement and fatigue. Many of us have a hard time asking for help, but people who do are more resilient and manage stress better. When others offer to help us, they typically genuinely mean it, and it's an opportunity for us to build relationships with them. People actually want to help us more than we realize.

Above all, God is our most valuable and powerful reserve for thriving in life. We can go to him for support from the first light of dawn until we lay our head down and then in the dark of night. He doesn't expect us to go through life or our parenting challenges with only our human strength and resources. Relying on his presence throughout the day and turning to him for his ever-present help lowers stress and anxiety.

He wants to help us just like we want to help our children when they're struggling and getting frustrated. But we have to trust him and believe in his goodness and power. We can depend on him to give us physical, mental, emotional, and spiritual renewal. Every time we call his name and wait expectantly, he answers. When we're weary from helping with homework, giving baths, and cleaning up, he can infuse us with a boost of new energy, patience, and joy. He may even help us in ways we don't expect. God not only sustains us; he raises us up to soar almost effortlessly and swiftly like eagles.

Dependence on God is a daily, hourly, and continual process of returning our attention to him and asking for his help throughout the day. C. S. Lewis wrote, "Relying on God has to begin all over again every day as if nothing had yet been done." Every time we trust God, it deepens our relationship with him.

So exchange your exhaustion for rejuvenation. With each breath, inhale God's power and exhale your weakness. Inhale Jesus's refreshment and exhale your weariness. Inhale the Spirit's joy and exhale your discouragement. Breathe in deeply and exhale completely.

Pray

I look to you, Jesus, for my strength. I wait for you to fill me with renewed energy and hope. Your presence rejuvenates my spirit and your joy lifts me up.

Ponder 3 MINUTES

Take a few minutes to record your thoughts.

1. In what ways are you weary?

---

2. What situations are you trying to manage in your own strength?

---

3. What's stopping you from asking for help from others and from God?

Practice 5 MINUTES

Depend on God's power.

1. Begin by taking two slow, deep breaths.

2. To your comfort level, lower your head, tuck in your arms, and lean over. Tense your body.

3. Focus on how you feel in the present moment.

4. Turn your attention to God. Whisper this prayer: "Lord, I trust you to help me."

5. Now rise up tall. Gaze upward, outstretch your arms, and open your hands. Pray: "You renew my strength."

Plan

Seek resiliency in God.

1. Memorize this line from Nehemiah 8:10: "The joy of the LORD is your strength!"

2. When you notice yourself feeling tired, stand up if you are able, gaze upward, and outstretch your arms.

3. Pray: "Your joy, Lord, is my strength." Wait expectantly for God to revive you.

REMEMBER

Look to Jesus for renewed strength.

DAY 35

Break Out of Darkness

If I say, "Surely the darkness shall cover me,
and night wraps itself around me,"
even the darkness is not dark to you.

—Psalm 139:11–12, NRSVUE

The unwelcome morning light peeked through the curtains, trying to brighten my thoughts. But I didn't have the strength to peel off the heavy blanket of melancholy or the desire to get out of bed.

"Morning, Mama! Mama . . . Mama?" The voices of my children pulled me out of my mental haze. Moving in slow motion, I got up and began the morning routine.

I struggled through my days for over a year. Then I became worse. My mental health spiral and disillusionment with God collided, sucking me into a swirling vortex of anger and despair. God was allowing my daughter to suffer and our family to fall apart. The chronic stress and grief had become more than I could handle. I couldn't lift myself out.

After a very dark season, I grew determined to recover, but I knew I couldn't heal on my own. I needed a lot of help from my family, friends, and church community; and I reached out to my pastor, therapist, psychiatrist, and physician. Then I committed to rising up and embracing life, even in the middle of my hopeless storm.

One evening not long after, Todd bolted into the house. "Come outside! Quick!"

The kids and I ran out into the wet grass with bare feet. We stood gazing in wonderment at the double rainbow streaming from one side of our house to the other. A burst of sunbeams had broken through the dark storm clouds, reflecting God's promise of new hope and his delight for me and my family.

If you feel overwhelmed, you're in the company of almost 50 percent of parents in the U.S. who say they have a hard time functioning on most days. Parents' mental health has significantly declined over recent years. A higher percentage of mothers report an *increase* in poor or fair mental health and a *decrease* in excellent mental health. Maybe most concerning is that 40 percent of teens are worried about the mental health of at least one of their parents. What's more, our mental health directly affects our children's mental health.

With the daily stress you're under, it would make sense if you're struggling with discouragement, a low mood, or depression. You're still a good parent, and your depression is not caused by a weak faith in God. Sarah J. Robinson has a message for you: "Sweet friend, there is nothing wrong with you. You are not a bad Christian for toiling under the crushing weight of depression. Mental illness is not a failure of faith or evidence of a flimsy prayer life."

You might also be feeling spiritually discouraged, distant from God, or abandoned by God. That's because mental health and faith are interlaced. Spiritual struggles can worsen mental health symptoms, and mental health decline can intensify faith problems. Strengthening your mental health and faith go hand in hand.

Some of us may face even more serious conditions like depression, bipolar disorder, and other disorders. Mental health disorders are a medical, chemical imbalance just like any other medical condition and often require medication and possibly long-term treatment. Sometimes mental health recovery takes a combination of professional therapy, pastoral counseling, medications, Christian community, and additional effective coping skills.

Sadness may gently tug at your mind and slow you down, or depression might be tightly wrapping its grip around you, making the darkness feel like it's going to swallow you up. But there is nowhere you can go out of the reach of God's Spirit and presence (see Psalm 139:7–10). In the pitch-black depths, even there Jesus is holding your hand, ready to pull you out from spiritual despair. He won't leave you there.

When it feels like darkness surrounds you, God is all around you, above you, below you, and inside you. Jesus loves you and will equip others to reach out to help you. His light beams behind the dark clouds, even when you cannot see it. God's radiant dawn vanquishes the terrifying night. Welcome the light of his Spirit. Let him in. Clasp Jesus's hand and break out of the darkness.

Pray

Jesus, you can light up my darkness. I open my heart, mind, and soul to let you in. Help me restore my mental health and faith in you.

Ponder 4 MINUTES

Take a few minutes to record your thoughts.

1. List any concerns you have about your mental health.

2. Describe any ways you're struggling in your faith.

3. How might your faith and mental health issues be interconnected?

4. Name any hesitations or obstacles in the way of your seeking mental health or spiritual help.

Practice 3 MINUTES

Open yourself to let God's light in.

1. Begin by taking two slow, deep breaths.

2. Picture yourself in a situation in which you typically feel overwhelmed mentally, emotionally, and/or spiritually.

3. Recite this prayer four times:

> *If I think surely the darkness will cover me,*
> *the darkness is as light to you, Lord.*

Plan

Strengthen your faith and mental health.

Take one of these steps to reach out for support this week.

- Speak to a pastoral counselor.
- Find a therapist.
- See your physician.
- Talk to a trusted friend.

*Please see the mental health resources in the back of the book on page 227.

REMEMBER

Welcome the Light in.

SEEK HELP

If you have mental health symptoms, please seek a professional consultation as soon as possible. If you are experiencing a crisis, call or text 988 or go to your closest emergency department.

Part 8

Cultivating a New Perspective

DAY 36

Laugh More

A happy heart is like good medicine,
but a broken spirit drains your strength.

—Proverbs 17:22, NCV

Thump! The blue exercise ball soared over the roof. I leapt off the swing and dashed to the makeshift first base. While Todd retrieved the ball, Bethany Grace began pumping her legs.

He sprinted back through the gate with the giant ball and moved up close to Bethany Grace. "Get ready . . . okay, here it comes . . ."

She let out one of her giggle squeals as the ball ricocheted off her legs. Dragging her toes to stop herself, she hopped off and ran toward me. Crashing into me, she grabbed my arms in gleeful laughter and pulled us to the ground. Her delight spread through all of us.

Our family spent much of the two summers of the COVID-19 pandemic in our backyard. To break up the monotony of sweltering days, we used our imaginations to invent several new silly games including "bubble trampoline," swimming pool "gator baseball," and—

our favorite creation—"swing kickball." During that stressful season, laughs didn't just spontaneously happen. We *made* them happen. Memories of those merry afternoons still make me chuckle.

The pressure we're under is making us sick. That's why we have to do something to lighten up our physical tension and mood. We have to laugh more. We have to seek joy more.

I was astounded by the abundance of research findings on the dramatic short-term and long-term physical and mental health benefits of laughter. It made me pay attention. Intentionally laughing more can be a healing balm for many of our emotional, mental, physical, and spiritual ills. Adding more humor to our daily lives can make us and our families more resilient.

Laughter reduces stress and improves mental and physical health. Humor triggers the release of mood-boosting chemicals like dopamine, oxytocin, and endorphins and improves circulation by pumping more oxygenated blood throughout the body. Laughing relaxes the mind and body and reduces muscle tension. Following laughing, there's a decrease in respiration rate, heart rate, blood pressure, and anxiety. Laughter also strengthens the immune system by lowering the production of stress hormones. Just a single session of laughter can reduce the level of the stress hormone cortisol by 37 percent. And it doesn't matter what causes you to laugh or how long you laugh.

Approaching life and parenting with a humorous disposition also improves the quality of our relationships and family functioning, including deeper bonds with our children, increased flexibility, and more creative problem-solving. Laughter changes our perspective and adds greater fun and joy to life. American poet E. E. Cummings is quoted as saying, "The most wasted of all days is one without laughter."

Lightheartedness is a learned skill for many, and most people laugh less the older they get. Children laugh approximately four hundred times a day, while the average adult chuckles only about fifteen times a day. Let's laugh more—the kind of laughter that brings joy and builds ourselves and others up.

But how do we laugh more when life doesn't feel funny?

We can put humorous reminders in front of us like downloading a laughter meditation app, purchasing a joke of the day desk calendar, or subscribing to a funny podcast. You could even try laughter yoga, which combines deep breathing, stretching, and simulated laughing. We can surround ourselves with others who have a good sense of humor and who laugh often. Laughter is contagious. Simply watching others laugh can tickle us, and we can make others laugh by sharing a funny joke or video or finding humor in a situation.

We can also cause the physical reaction that will make us laugh. Our emotions often follow our physiological responses. William James, one of the founders of psychology, is quoted as saying, "We don't laugh because we're happy. We're happy because we laugh." In other words, our brain takes cues from our body, which influences how we feel emotionally. We can begin by fake laughing. Self-induced laughter can actually be even more effective at reducing stress and improving our health than spontaneous laughter.

A happy heart and cheery countenance are medicine for the soul. God delights in our enjoyment of life, especially when we share it with others. When we mindfully live in the moment, we see more opportunities for laughing. Janet Holm McHenry wrote, "God brings laughter into our lives; we just need to look for its opportunity."

Where in your day can you laugh and more deeply enjoy life? Throughout your day, look for opportunities to encourage childlike glee to well up and spill out in laughter.

Pray

Jesus, thank you for the gift of laughter. Help me look for more ways I can enjoy life and make others laugh and smile too.

Ponder 2 MINUTES

Take a few minutes to record your thoughts.

1. What makes you laugh?

2. What's one easy way you can add laughter breaks to your day?

Practice 3 MINUTES

Make yourself laugh.

Look at yourself in a mirror or on your phone.

1. Begin by taking two slow, deep breaths.
2. Hold your stomach and inhale a deep breath while smiling at yourself. Exhale.
3. Inhale and smile bigger. As you exhale, quietly giggle.
4. Now slowly begin laughing. Gradually laugh faster and louder.

Plan

Schedule a laughter break.

Plan a time today to watch funny videos, look at amusing memes, read or watch a comedy, talk to a friend who makes you laugh, or do another humorous activity.

REMEMBER

Laugh more often.

DAY 37

Plan Fun Activities

I recommend having fun, because there is nothing better for people in this world than to eat, drink, and enjoy life. That way they will experience some happiness along with all the hard work God gives them under the sun.

—Ecclesiastes 8:15

I stared at the mocking cursor blinking on my laptop screen. As the firm deadline for my major work project drew closer, the weight of stress pressed harder on my attention. My overwrought mind begged for relief.

My phone dinged. A text from Todd. "How's it going?"

I let out a groan and typed back: "It's not. I'm so stressed out."

Todd: "Let's plan something fun you can look forward to."

I perked up. "That sounds good. What do you have in mind?"

Todd: "We've all talked about wanting to go see a movie. Sunday?"

"That sounds wonderful." I added some smiling heart emojis. Todd had known just what I needed.

I stared at my laptop screen and said a prayer. Then my fingers started to tap on the keys, then skip and hop. Those plans gave me the mental boost I needed to ride the rising stress, not merely slog through it. My thoughts cleared and the tension let up. I was able to focus for the next four days.

We hadn't been to the theater as a family in over a year, which had been way too long. After getting over our shock at the cost of tickets, we entered the lobby. The sound of popcorn popping and the aroma of salty butter made my mouth water. Excited to take my seat, I pushed the button to recline my chair. With my popcorn bucket in my lap, I looked to my left and right at my family beside me. The corners of my mouth turned up in pure delight as the previews began.

As we've been discovering, living mindfully in the present moment can be a powerful stress-reduction tool. Sometimes, though, we need to plan and anticipate positive future events. Looking forward to an enjoyable outing, especially with a set date, helps us psychologically by boosting our mood and buffering the strain of stress. Imagining a fun activity releases dopamine, a neurotransmitter that makes us feel pleasure and happiness. Brainstorming and planning also increases our optimism about the future, deepens our enjoyment of life, and strengthens our relationship bonds. Simply put, taking time for fun gives us a mental and physical break and prevents burnout.

Scheduling fun into your daily routine could be as small as watching a funny movie in the evening, going to dinner with friends, organizing a family activity on the weekend, or even scheduling a vacation for six months away. Planning both enjoyable activities during the week and bigger events throughout the year are necessary for healthy parents and families. A daily fun routine might include keeping a joke book or interactive silly story activity at the family dinner table or playing silly songs and dancing while you clean up. Making time for an activity you enjoy can also add an important dose of fun to your week. Perhaps you enjoy a certain type of physical exercise like biking or yoga, a hobby such as woodworking or crocheting, or an activity such as reading. Schedule these types of fun moments into your day whenever you can.

And don't underestimate spontaneous moments of fun either. Celebrate life with your family often and do something special for small victories like when a child does their best on a test or plays hard in a soccer game, or you turn in a project at work. Bake a sweet treat to celebrate just because.

Living lightheartedly and having fun is also spiritual. God wants us to enjoy life and not just trudge through the demands of the day or week or month. He created us to work hard, glorify him, and share his truth and love with others, but also to rest, play, and have fun. Kevin Gushiken wrote, "Should we not play in beautiful and celebratory ways in response to God's work in our lives? . . . Play for Christians is not an escape from the challenges of life but an attitude of celebration, even in the midst of life's difficulties. Play is not carefree living but purposeful enjoyment of life."

Imagine ways you can add more fun to your days. Laugh, smile, and enjoy life to the fullest.

Pray

Jesus, give me a lighthearted spirit and help me to see opportunities to enjoy the abundant life you've given me.

Ponder 3 MINUTES

Take a few minutes to record your thoughts.

1. What types of activities are fun for you and your family that you don't do very often?

2. What's one mini activity you can schedule into your week?

3. Name one bigger event you would like to plan.

Practice 3 MINUTES

Plan a fun break.

1. Begin by taking two slow, deep breaths.

2. Think about one of the activities you enjoy that you've stopped making time for.

3. Brainstorm possible times and places you could take a break this week and spend fifteen to twenty minutes on the activity.

4. Schedule this time and enjoy your fun break.

Plan

Take time for fun.

Be on the lookout for ways you can add more enjoyment to your week with your family and friends and for opportunities when you can take fun breaks yourself.

REMEMBER

Plan more fun and enjoy life to the fullest.

DAY 38

Move in Gratitude

Give thanks to the LORD, for he is good!
His faithful love endures forever.
—1 Chronicles 16:34

I spread out my art supplies on the kitchen table. Choosing a pair of scalloped scissors, I began creating different colored cards. Next, I made a chart. In the middle of the poster board, I wrote, "Prayer Requests," and at the top, "Thank you, God, for answered prayers." Last, I attached an envelope for keeping the blank cards handy.

Now it was time for the kids to help. First we needed some fun music to work to. Then we all picked markers and drew pictures to decorate our new prayer board. We chose the wall across from the family dinner table and excitedly tacked up our poster.

Each day, as we thought of a prayer request, we wrote it on a card and stuck it to the bottom of the board. We prayed for the little girls next door whose mother was sick with cancer, for friends at school, for family members, and for people at church. We also wrote cards asking God to provide for our family. Each night at dinner, we checked the board, prayed for some of the requests, and thanked God for the answered prayers.

Every time God answered one of our prayers, we moved the card up to the top and thanked him. Pretty soon, the top of the board was overflowing and there was plenty of room on the bottom. Thanking God became a regular habit, central to our family life. During those same years, the kids often danced to joyful music in the kitchen. Looking back, I see that their dancing was very fitting.

One of the most life-changing habits we can develop is practicing gratitude. Expressing thanks increases our positive emotions, improves our ability to cope with stress, makes us more resilient, and betters our overall mental well-being. Showing appreciation to others also strengthens and enhances our relationships. Saying thank you to someone else lifts their spirits as well as our own. Thanking God, whether privately in prayer or out loud where others can hear, is the utmost act of gratitude and a powerful force in our lives. Specifically, regularly journaling prayers of thanksgiving to God is linked with a decrease in stress, depression, anxiety, physical health symptoms, and even hemoglobin A1c in women, which indicates healthier blood sugar control.

When we keep our focus on how God is working in our lives and in our families, our trust in his abiding faithfulness deepens. We begin to see blessings right in front of us and all around us. Giving thanks on a daily basis leads us in the rhythm of moving through life to the tune of a grateful heart. Expressing gratitude shifts our perspective to a more positive outlook on life and gives us fresh hope. In Lisa Appelo's words, "Gratitude is the gateway to joy and helps us find contentment right where we are." We don't have to look any further than the present moment to see God's amazing blessings. He creates personalized gifts for us that are more marvelous than anything we could ever imagine or ask for. God is in those moments when your child snuggles up close to you, your family laughs together at dinnertime, or you find the perfect gift for a friend. And when we accept his generosity, we become overwhelmed with gratitude and a desire to do good things and be generous to others.

Thanking God is an act of worship. The psalmist wrote, "I will give thanks and praise the LORD, with all my heart; I will tell aloud all Your wonders and marvelous deeds" (Psalm 9:1, AMP). When we praise and thank God, he opens our eyes and reveals more of his glory to us. We realize all that we already have, we desire less, and we want to thank him more. Oh, he is so, so good! We need only look at all the blessings he has given our families to realize how much we have to be grateful for.

Get swept up in thanking God and rejoicing in his majestic presence. Move your heart to the melody of gratefulness and dance to the rhythm of gratitude. Express your thankfulness for his gracious love, and he will fill you with unending joy.

Pray

Lord Jesus, you have been so good to me. I thank you with all my heart for your faithful love, your marvelous works in my life, and your blessings in my family. All the glory is yours.

Ponder 2 MINUTES

Take a few minutes to record your thoughts.

1. How often do you express gratitude?

---

2. What are some of the different ways you could thank God and show appreciation to others?

Practice 4 MINUTES

Praise God with thanksgiving.

1. Begin by taking two slow, deep breaths.
2. Name all that you're thankful for. Let your thoughts flow.
3. Pick a few blessings from your list.
4. Praise God for all he's done: "Lord, I thank you with all my heart for ______________."
5. Continue growing your gratitude list as you go about your day.

Plan

Develop the habit of practicing gratitude.

1. Brainstorm more ways you can express gratitude to others and thank God more often. Some ideas include:

   Create a family thankfulness board.

   Start a notebook and list your blessings.

   Leave little thank-you notes for others.

   Write a social media post thanking and praising God.

2. Choose one and begin this week.

REMEMBER

Let your heart dance to the rhythm of gratitude.

DAY 39

Discover Beauty

One thing I ask from the LORD,
this only do I seek:
that I may dwell in the house of the LORD
all the days of my life,
to gaze on the beauty of the LORD
and to seek him in his temple.
—Psalm 27:4, NIV

I stepped out into the fresh air and began walking to the park. When I reached the quiet brook, I strolled along the water. The softly flowing stream captured my thoughts, and I stopped to sit on a wooden bench. I admired the trail of white trillium flowers running along the water's edge. The sweet fragrance from trumpet-shaped honeysuckle calmed me. A blue swallowtail butterfly flittered on a leaf nearby. The sun warmed my face as a gentle breeze whistled through the trees and rustled my hair.

I soaked in the tranquil scenery. Then it occurred to me that I was actually gazing upon a hint of God's splendor. As I breathed in deeply,

God's breath became my own. I lingered, marveling at his beauty and enjoying his peaceful presence. My work at home urged me to head back, while God's Spirit nudged me to remain in his sanctuary a little while longer. I sat captivated, giving in to my soul's desire—to see more of his beauty and to know him in deeper ways.

I've learned that rushing through my day to get everything done draws my focus away from my present surroundings. This can cause me to miss seeing the sweetest moments and the loveliness in my children and others. On the flip side, approaching my day with a spirit of curiosity and expectation can open my eyes to discover beauty where I least expect it.

When we remain fully awake to our environment as well as in tune with our thoughts and feelings, we develop a heightened awareness and can perceive beauty with all our senses. Practicing mindfulness and deep breathing opens our heart and mind to enjoy life on a deeper level, to create richer memories, and to feel more pleasant and relaxed.

When a person stands in an art museum fascinated by a painting, they study every detail to learn about the artist through their masterpiece. In the same way, when we gaze at a magnificent mountain view or watch our precious child sleeping, we are really admiring a reflection of God's image, love, and goodness. And these moments make us long to experience more of his beauty. Steve DeWitt described it this way: "God is the object of our beauty cravings. As the beauty beyond and behind all created beauty, He is the measure of what is truly beautiful."

Many people sense God's presence and beauty in nature. But his exquisite design surrounds us in every moment, in our homes, and anywhere we go. If we listen carefully, we can witness his lovely Spirit in our children's singing or see his creativity in their drawings. Beauty reveals a hint of the mystery of God's grace and provides evidence of where his paintbrush has touched. He creates a serene landscape or spectacular ocean sunset for us to enjoy and for him to display part of himself.

The whole earth is filled with his glory (see Isaiah 6:3), but he only shows us a reflection, because his majesty is more than we could ever take in. In seeking God's presence, we discover glimpses of his glory. Just one encounter of his wondrous presence can forever change us. We fall in love with him and want to experience his depths more.

In moments when beauty captivates us, God is wooing us to himself. He's composing a love song to us. I can only attempt to describe to you my own wordless experience, for how God showers me with surprise lavish gifts is different from how he's pursuing you. He delights in you and uniquely created you to experience his beauty in different ways. I pray that you will experience his pure beauty and love and that you will encounter Jesus, God on earth. Whatever draws you to desiring God more, embark on a quest to experience those sources of beauty.

Discover beauty in every moment of your day, in every breath you take, right where you are—in your child's smile, through the affection in your home, and in all the places you go. You can also simply whisper the name of Jesus to enter the magnificent palace of his presence and find yourself surrounded in splendor. Linger there in the sweet fragrance of his love, gazing at his radiance. Get lost in his beauty and fall deeper in love with him, and he will fill you with the resplendent joy of life.

Pray

Jesus, you're beautiful. There's no one like you. Open my heart to know you more and my eyes to see your magnificent handiwork everywhere I go.

Ponder 3 MINUTES

Take a few minutes to record your thoughts.

1. What captivates you?

2. Where have you seen God's beauty?

3. How can you seek to experience his presence in deeper ways?

Practice 5–10 MINUTES

Discover beauty all around you.

1. Begin by taking two slow, deep breaths.
2. Sit mindfully or go for a mindful prayer walk.
3. As you sit or stroll, silently observe your surroundings with all your senses.
4. Ask God to show you his beauty and expect to find glimpses of his marvelousness.
5. Delight in his presence.

Plan

Look for beauty.

As you go about your week, continue to seek beauty and catch glimpses of God's brilliance.

REMEMBER

Discover God's beauty wherever you are.

DAY 40

Treasure Simple Moments

This is the day that the LORD has made;
let us rejoice and be glad in it.
—Psalm 118:24, ESV

Bethany Grace curled up under my arm as we snuggled on our new porch swing. Dusk was disappearing into the clear night sky.

"What dat?" She sat up and pointed.

I followed her enthralled gaze to the faint flickers. "Fireflies, honey. They're fireflies!"

The delight in her eyes sparked joy in my spirit. From our front-row seat, we watched the lightning bugs come out on stage to dance around the yard. I marveled at her anticipation for the next one to flash. Then the next. Every time, her face lit up like the glow from the bug, and so did mine. It dawned on me that we had never really stopped before to just sit and watch fireflies.

As the night grew darker, the sparks flashed brighter. We could no longer see each other's faces, but we enjoyed each other's joy, fully absorbed in that precious moment in time as everything else faded away. Like a special event caught on camera and framed on the wall in our home, that simple moment will forever be a priceless memory. That evening, heaven joined us and showed me the gift of treasuring simple moments.

Many of us go through life waiting for big moments like giving birth, adopting, or watching our children reach new milestones. We look forward to special occasions such as weddings and holidays or amazing experiences of trips and new adventures. But these events are few and far between and oftentimes are stressful and don't live up to our expectations. We experience only a hint of the enjoyment of life when we spend time thinking about the future or going over the past. If we're always looking ahead or back, we can easily miss the most important moments of our lives right in front of us.

Practicing mindfulness every day helps us recognize opportunities to create special memories. But to notice these priceless gems, we have to be living in the present moment. The times we slow down to enjoy life with our children, friends, and loved ones are the days we will remember most. We store up these little golden nuggets, and they become the most precious treasures of our lives.

When we live in the present, we're more aware of our thoughts, emotions, and bodily sensations. We're able to maintain more focused attention, think on a deeper level, feel emotions more intensely, and have more meaningful conversations and connections with others. We also become more observant of our surroundings with our senses. Our experiences of smells, tastes, touches, sights, and sounds are richer, which makes our experiences more pleasant. We form more vivid memories, and when we are fully living in the here and now, it can actually feel like time has slowed down.

God has created this very day as a gift for us to enjoy. We honor God when we make the conscious choice to fully live in today in gratitude for a new morning. Let's celebrate this day and look for all the blessings God has added in. As Tama Fortner prayed, "If only I have eyes to see all the everyday blessings found here at the intersection of ordinary and divine." Just like a fleeting sunrise will never be the same, this exact minute and our different moments with our children will never come again. But God always remains the same. It is him there in the moment that makes it divine.

This day that God has made is full of joyful happenings just waiting to be discovered. If you're looking, you will find them, because God is everywhere. Whatever moment you're in, be fully there. Create a special memory today. Then another one tomorrow. Immerse yourself in the present and hear whispers of God's wonder. He delights in you, and he's telling you, "You are my beloved, and I cherish you." Pause. Just breathe. Just be. Rest here where heaven is meeting you now, in this present moment.

Pray

Jesus, I treasure this moment with you right now. Give me the gift of seeing simple moments and teach me to capture them in my heart.

Ponder 2 MINUTES

Take a few minutes to record your thoughts.

1. What are some special memories you treasure most?

2. How can you and your family slow down and treasure simple moments in your day?

Practice 5 MINUTES

Rejoice in this moment.

1. Begin by taking two slow, deep breaths.
2. Be fully present in each breath you take. Inhale. Exhale.
3. Look inward and all around. Where do you see gifts from God?
4. Celebrate the day and all the blessings with which God has filled it.
5. Treasure this moment.

Plan

Make special memories.

Slow down this week and look for opportunities to share special moments with your child and loved ones.

REMEMBER

Treasure simple moments.

Helpful Resources

Mental Health

- **Crisis Lifeline:** Call or text 988, https://988lifeline.org
- **Find a therapist:** www.psychologytoday.com/us/therapists
- **Christian counselor locator:** https://christiancareconnect.com
- **National Institute of Health:** "My Mental Health: Do I Need Help?" www.nimh.nih.gov/health/publications/my-mental-health-do-i-need-help
- **Cleveland Clinic:** "Anxiety Disorders," https://my.clevelandclinic.org/health/diseases/9536-anxiety-disorders
- **Disability Parenting:** Mental Health Resources, https://disabilityparenting.com/mental-health

Christian Mindfulness Guided Meditations

- **Abide:** https://abide.com

- **Calming Grace:** www.calminggrace.com/christian-mindfulness-resources/#meditations
- **Calming Christian:** www.youtube.com/@CalmingChristian

Acknowledgments

God has written my life's story, and it is only through his remarkable love and grace I am the person and writer I am today. He has given me others to guide and teach me along the way, and I was able to write this book because of all those who have loved and supported me over the years.

This book would not exist were it not for the incredible love of my husband and his cheerleading my writing. Thank you, Todd, for helping me chase my dreams and for letting me steal away to the office for hours on end. To my children who inspire me and gave up time with Mama so I could write, thank you for this gift. I am forever grateful to my parents for their unending love and support. Thank you, Mom and Dad, for nurturing my dream of writing since I was a child and for coming to care for the kids so I could focus on the book. I also appreciate the encouragement and support from my father-in-law. Thank you, Grandpa, for coming to care for the kids and help Todd so I could work.

Life would not be as rich without my friends who have been there with me through all the seasons of life, from relishing meals together and laughing for hours to sitting with me and sharing my pain and tears. Thank you for the blessing of your friendship and for the ways you are a special part of my story. I would like to thank the counselors and therapists who have patiently walked this road with me and also my graduate school professors and professional supervisors who taught me how to care for the hearts and minds and souls of others. Thank you, everyone, for helping create this book and for making it possible.

Notes

Dear Parent

ix **About half of parents in America:** Office of the Surgeon General (OSG), "Parents Under Pressure: The U.S. Surgeon General's Advisory on the Mental Health & Well-Being of Parents," U.S. Department of Health and Human Services (2024): 9, www.ncbi.nlm.nih.gov/books/NBK606662/.

ix **But excess stress can cascade:** "Stress Effects on the Body," American Psychological Association, last reviewed October 21, 2024, www.apa.org/topics/stress/body.

ix **Over time, chronic stress increases:** Bruce S. McEwen, "Neurobiological and Systemic Effects of Chronic Stress," *Chronic Stress* 1 (2017): 1, https://journals.sagepub.com/doi/10.1177/2470547017692328.

xi **Studies have shown the powerful faith:** Kristy Ford and Fernando Garzon, "Research Note: A Randomized Investigation of Evangelical Christian Accommodative Mindfulness," *Spirituality in Clinical Practice* 4, no. 2 (2017): 92, https://doi.org/10.1037/scp0000137; Veronica L. Timbers and Jennifer C. Hollenberger, "Christian Mindfulness and Mental Health: Coping through Sacred Traditions and Embodied Awareness," *Religions* 13, no. 1 (2022): 5, https://doi.org/10.3390/rel13010062.

Day 1: Focus on One Moment

4 **But multitasking is a myth:** Kevin P. Madore and Anthony D. Wagner, "Multicosts of Multitasking," *Cerebrum: the Dana Forum on Brain Science* (2019): 1–2, https://pubmed.ncbi.nlm.nih.gov/32206165.

4 **In doing so, we actually accomplish 40 percent less:** Suzanne K. Powell, "Mindfulness, Multitasking, and You," *Professional Case Management* 21, no. 2 (2016): 61–62, https://pubmed.ncbi.nlm.nih.gov/26844712/.

4 **Task switching raises our stress levels:** Jennifer E. Davis, "Multitasking and How It Affects Your Brain Health," Brown University Health, January 26, 2023, www.brownhealth.org/be-well/multitasking-and-how-it-affects-your-brain-health.

4 **Our brains simply are not designed:** Menno Nijboer et al., "Single-Task fMRI Overlap Predicts Concurrent Multitasking Interference," *NeuroImage* 100, no. 15 (2014): 60, https://doi.org/10.1016/j.neuroimage.2014.05.082; Davis, "Multitasking."

4 ***Mindfulness* is simply staying in the:** Nijboer et al., "Single-Task fMRI."

4 **"The shorter way to do many":** This quote is often attributed to Wolfgang Amadeus Mozart, but there is actually no definitive historical source or record of the quote.

5 **Yet finding ways to single task:** Yi-Yuan Tang et al., "The Neuroscience of Mindfulness Meditation," *Nature Reviews Neuroscience* 16, no. 4 (2015): 213, https://doi.org/10.1038/nrn3916.

Day 2: Just Breathe

9 **When we feel stressed, we typically:** Better Health Channel, "Breathing to Reduce Stress," Victoria State Government Department of Health, accessed May 1, 2025, www.betterhealth.vic.gov.au/health/healthyliving/breathing-to-reduce-stress.

9 **Observing our breath is the most:** Ravinder Jerath et al., "Self-Regulation of Breathing as a Primary Treatment for Anxiety," *Applied Psychophysiology and Biofeedback* 40, no. 2 (2015): 112, https://doi.org/10.1007/s10484-015-9279-8.

9 **By practicing diaphragmatic breathing:** Valentin Magnon et al., "Benefits from One Session of Deep and Slow Breathing on Vagal Tone and Anxiety in Young and Older Adults," *Scientific Reports* 11 (September 2021): 6, https://doi.org/10.1038/s41598-021-98736-9.

9 **And exhaling slightly longer than inhaling:** Christopher Bergland, "Longer Exhalations Are an Easy Way to Hack Your Vagus Nerve," Psychology Today,

updated May 20, 2024, www.psychologytoday.com/us/blog/the-athletes-way/201905/longer-exhalations-are-an-easy-way-to-hack-your-vagus-nerve.

10 **"Let the remembrance of Jesus be":** Saint John Climacus, *The Ladder of Divine Ascent* (Paulist Press, 1982), 48.

10 **While drawing us closer to God:** Shingo Ueda, "The Neurobiological Link Between Prayer, Breath Control and Serotonin Release," *International Journal of Science and Research Archive* 13, no. 2 (2024): 631–34, https://doi.org/10.30574/ijsra.2024.13.2.2136.

10 **"The science of breathing and the":** Jennifer Tucker, *Breath as Prayer* (Thomas Nelson, 2022), 19.

Day 3: Remain in Today

14 **Worrying about the future triggers our:** "Understanding the Stress Response: Chronic Activation of This Survival Mechanism Impairs Health," Harvard Health Publishing, April 3, 2024, www.health.harvard.edu/staying-healthy/understanding-the-stress-response.

15 **"Some people spend so much time":** Franklin Graham, *Billy Graham in Quotes* (Thomas Nelson, 2011), 378.

15 **Remaining in the present calms those:** Yi-Yuan Tang et al., "The Neuroscience of Mindfulness Meditation," *Nature Reviews Neuroscience* 16, no. 4 (2015): 222, https://doi.org/10.1038/nrn3916.

15 **We instead use the areas of:** Jason N. Linder, "5 Ways Mindfulness Practice Positively Changes Your Brain: Recent Research Shows How Mindfulness Rewires Our Brain for Calm and Well-Being," Psychology Today, May 9, 2019, www.psychologytoday.com/us/blog/mindfulness-insights/201905/5-ways-mindfulness-practice-positively-changes-your-brain.

15 **"paying attention to the present moment":** Regina Chow Trammel and John Trent, *A Counselor's Guide to Christian Mindfulness: Engaging the Mind, Body & Soul in Biblical Practices & Therapies* (Zondervan Reflective, 2021), 17.

15 **"Christ-centered present moment awareness":** Everett L. Worthington Jr. et al., eds., *Evidence-Based Practices for Christian Counseling and Psychotherapy* (IVP Academic, 2013), 65.

Day 4: Accept the Present

19 **Practicing acceptance can reduce your body's:** Emily K. Lindsay et al., "Acceptance Lowers Stress Reactivity: Dismantling Mindfulness Training in a Randomized Controlled Trial," *Psychoneuroendocrinology* 87 (2018): 70, https://doi.org/10.1016/j.psyneuen.2017.09.015.

19 **When you truly accept your present:** Marsha M. Linehan, *DBT Skills Training Manual,* 2nd ed. (The Guilford Press, 2015), 453.

20 **"Joy is not necessarily the absence":** Sam Storms, *Pleasures Evermore: The Life-Changing Power of Enjoying God* (NavPress, 2000), 52.

20 **"God has yet to bless anyone":** Dallas Willard, *The Divine Conspiracy: Rediscovering Our Hidden Life in God* (HarperCollins, 1997), 348–49.

Day 5: Parent Mindfully

25 **Mindful parents tend to be more:** Larissa G. Duncan et al., "A Model of Mindful Parenting: Implications for Parent–Child Relationships and Prevention Research," *Clinical Child and Family Psychology Review* 12, no. 3 (2009): 261, 263, https://doi.org/10.1007/s10567-009-0046-3; Alicia Bazzano et al., "Mindfulness Based Stress Reduction (MBSR) for Parents and Caregivers of Individuals with Developmental Disabilities: A Community-Based Approach," *Journal of Child and Family Studies* 24 (2015): 299, https://doi.org/10.1007/s10826-013-9836-9.

25 **Parenting mindfully can help us reduce:** Jon Kabat-Zinn and Myla Kabat-Zinn, "Mindful Parenting: Perspectives on the Heart of the Matter," *Mindfulness* 12, no. 2 (2021): 266, https://doi.org/10.1007/s12671-020-01564-7.

Day 6: Leave Your Worries

32 **whereas anxiety is more intense, persistent:** Sadaf Munir and Veronica Takov, "Generalized Anxiety Disorder," National Institute of Health, National Library of Medicine, National Center for Biotechnology Information, last updated October 17, 2022, www.ncbi.nlm.nih.gov/books/NBK441870.

32 **If you're experiencing moderate to severe:** Richard Weissbourd et al., "Caring for the Caregivers: The Critical Link Between Parent and Teen Mental

Health," Harvard University Graduate School of Education, June 2023, https://mcc.gse.harvard.edu/reports/caring-for-the-caregivers.

32 **Parents of children with any type of:** Nathaniel Scherer et al., "Depression and Anxiety in Parents of Children with Intellectual and Developmental Disabilities: A Systematic Review and Meta-Analysis," *PLoS One* 14, no. 7 (2019): 2, e0219888, https://doi.org/10.1371/journal.pone.0219888.

33 **"Anxiety is a signal alerting you":** Craig Groeschel, "Praying Through the Pain: Anxious for Nothing Part 2," sermon, Life Church, Edmond, Oklahoma, August 11, 2019, 7 min., 7 sec., www.life.church/media/anxious-for-nothing/praying-through-the-pain.

Day 7: Surrender Control

38 **attempting to control what we cannot:** Ariane Resnick, "Why Letting Go of Control Can Help You Enjoy Life," Verywell Mind, last updated on March 13, 2024, www.verywellmind.com/letting-go-of-control-can-help-you-enjoy-life-5208817#citation-9.

39 **"We can't stop or control things":** Lysa TerKeurst, "Nothing in life is certain," Facebook, October 7, 2022, www.facebook.com/OfficialLysa/photos/nothing-in-life-is-certain-unpredictable-circumstances-roll-in-and-out-like-the-/616753459817829/.

Day 8: Calm Your Body

43 **Extensive research has shown that engaging:** Syazwina Muhammad Khir et al., "Efficacy of Progressive Muscle Relaxation in Adults for Stress, Anxiety, and Depression: A Systematic Review," *Psychology Research and Behavior Management* 17 (2024): 361, https://doi.org/10.2147/PRBM.S437277.

43 **Listening to a PMR meditation can:** Katharine C. Simon et al., "Progressive Muscle Relaxation Increases Slow-Wave Sleep During a Daytime Nap," *Journal of Sleep Research* 31, no. 5 (2022): 2, https://pmc.ncbi.nlm.nih.gov/articles/PMC9786620/.

44 **"Progressive muscle relaxation infused with God's":** Regina Chow Trammel and John Trent, *A Counselor's Guide to Christian Mindfulness: Engaging the Mind, Body & Soul in Biblical Practices & Therapies* (Zondervan Reflective, 2021), 191.

44 **The Hebrew root word translated as** ***soul:*** *Zondervan NIV Study Bible* (Zondervan, 2002), 792, 937.

Day 9: Say No to Yes

48 **People who overcommit have higher levels:** Dorothea Margarete Hinsch et al., "Associations Between Overcommitment, Effort–Reward Imbalance and Mental Health: Findings from a Longitudinal Study," *International Archives of Occupational and Environmental Health* 92, no. 4 (2018): 5, https://doi.org/10.1007/s00420-018-1391-7.

48 **There are three main emotional reasons:** Israa Nasir, "Why You're Chronically Overcommitted," *Harvard Business Review,* January 6, 2025, https://hbr.org/2025/01/why-youre-chronically-overcommitted.

48 **And the more we say yes:** Sunita Sah, "Why We Say Yes When We Don't Want To," *Time,* January 4, 2025, https://time.com/7204326/saying-yes-instead-of-no-essay/.

49 **"The key is not to prioritize":** Stephen R. Covey, *The 7 Habits of Highly Effective People,* 4th ed. (Simon & Schuster, 2020), 183.

Day 10: Be Flexible

53 **Psychological flexibility involves being more open:** Todd B. Kashdan, "Psychological Flexibility as a Fundamental Aspect of Health," *Clinical Psychology Review* 30, no. 7 (2010): 866–68, https://pmc.ncbi.nlm.nih.gov/articles/PMC2998793.

54 **"not as annoyances, but as opportunities":** Tama Fortner, *Everyday Joys* (Ink & Willow, 2024), 73.

Day 11: Retreat to the Quiet

60 **Sensory overload causes stress on the:** Saundra Dalton-Smith, *Sacred Rest: Recover Your Life, Renew Your Energy, Restore Your Sanity* (FaithWords, 2017), 88–90.

60 **Studies have shown that isolating from:** Anette Kjellgren and Jessica Westman, "Beneficial Effects of Treatment with Sensory Isolation in Flotation-Tank as a Preventive Health-Care Intervention—A Randomized Controlled Pilot Trial," *BMC Complementary and Alternative Medicine* 14, no. 1 (2014): 2, 6, www.biomedcentral.com/1472-6882/14/417.

61 **"When we carve out space for":** Rebekah Lyons, *Rhythms of Renewal: Trading Stress and Anxiety for a Life of Peace and Purpose* (Zondervan, 2019), 47.

Day 12: Stop to Rest

65 **According to the Centers for Disease:** Amanda Blackwelder et al., "Effect of Inadequate Sleep on Frequent Mental Distress," *Preventing Chronic Disease* 18, no. 61 (2021): 1, www.cdc.gov/pcd/issues/2021/20_0573.htm.

65 **And almost half of us have:** "Stress and Sleep," American Psychological Association, accessed May 27, 2025, www.apa.org/news/press/releases/stress/2013/sleep.

65 **There's a strong correlation between:** "Stress and Sleep," American Psychological Association.

65 **Inadequate sleep also leads to:** Blackwelder et al., "Effect of Inadequate Sleep," 1.

65 **regular sleep helps our muscles relax:** Eric Suni, "What Happens When You Sleep?," *Sleep Foundation,* updated July 10, 2025, www.sleepfoundation.org/how-sleep-works/what-happens-when-you-sleep.

66 **"Sleep is different from rest":** Saundra Dalton-Smith, *Sacred Rest: Recover Your Life, Renew Your Energy, Restore Your Sanity* (FaithWords, 2017), 8.

66 **Go outside in the sunlight:** Rachel Salas, "A Day That Leads to Your Best Night's Sleep," John Hopkins Medicine, accessed May 27, 2025, www.hopkinsmedicine.org/health/wellness-and-prevention/a-day-that-leads-to-your-best-nights-sleep.

66 **Engage in some type of physical:** "8 Secrets to a Good Night's Sleep," Harvard Health, November 20, 2023, www.health.harvard.edu/newsletter_article/8-secrets-to-a-good-nights-sleep.

Day 13: Refresh Your Soul

71 **This practice is linked to significant:** Stephanie Reeves, "Release Stress with Transformative Bible Meditation," Abide, June 5, 2023, https://abide.com/blog/release-stress-with-transformative-bible-meditation; Paul Ratanasiripong and Sun Tsai, "Impact of Christian Meditation and Biofeedback on the Mental Health of Graduate Students in Seminary: A Pilot Study," *Insights on the Depression and Anxiety* 4 (2020): 20, 22–23.

72 **"Master's heart and mind." He wrote:** W. Phillip Keller, *A Shepherd Looks at Psalm 23: Discovering God's Love for You* (Zondervan, 2007), 62.

Day 14: Pray in Silence

76 **sitting in silent prayer helps calm:** Regina Chow Trammel and John Trent, *A Counselor's Guide to Christian Mindfulness: Engaging the Mind, Body & Soul in Biblical Practices & Therapies* (Zondervan Reflective, 2021), 50–51.

77 **"In the depths of our souls":** Tammie Southerland, *Wordless Prayer: How God Hears and Answers Your Groans and Tears* (Chosen, 2024), 20.

Day 15: Manage Technology

81 **A whopping 86 percent of Americans say:** American Psychological Association, *Stress in America: Coping with Change,* Stress in America™ Survey (American Psychological Association, 2017), 2, www.apa.org/news/press/releases/stress/2017/technology-social-media.pdf.

81 **The use of smartphones:** Jesper Pedersen et al., "Effects of Limiting Digital Screen Use on Well-Being, Mood, and Biomarkers of Stress in Adults," *npj Mental Health Research* 1, no. 1 (2022): 1, www.nature.com/articles/s44184-022-00015-6.

81 **The psychological term for this condition:** APA Dictionary of Psychology, "technostress," last updated April 19, 2018, https://dictionary.apa.org/technostress.

81 **when they're together, due to technology:** "Stress in America," American Psychological Association, 5.

82 **Reducing household screen time can significantly:** Pedersen et al., "Effects of Limiting Digital Screen Use," 2.

82 **After just two weeks of limiting:** Allison Aubrey, "A Break from Your Smartphone Can Reboot Your Mood. Here's How Long You Need," NPR, February 24, 2025, www.npr.org/2025/02/24/nx-s1-5304417/smartphone-break-digital-detox-screen-addiction.

82 **"How much of our stress response":** Barb Roose, *Stronger Than Stress: 10 Spiritual Practices to Win the Battle of Overwhelm* (Revell, 2024), 51.

Day 16: Lay Down Perfectionism

91 **"Healthy striving is self-focused":** Brené Brown, *The Gifts of Imperfection: Let Go of Who You Think You're Supposed to Be and Embrace Who You Are* (Hazelden, 2010), 56.

91 **Pediatrician and psychoanalyst D. W. Winnicott:** D. W. Winnicott, *Babies and Their Mothers,* ed. Clare Winnicott et al. (Perseus, 1987), 38.

91 **Good enough parents care for their:** Shwikar Othman et al., "Examining the Influence of Self-Compassion Education and Training Upon Parents and Families When Caring for Their Children: A Systematic Review," *The Open Psychology Journal* 15, no. 1 (2022): 14, http://dx.doi.org/10.2174/18743501-v15-e221020-2022-39.

Day 17: Trade Busyness for Simplicity

95 **Parenting and family burnout also spills:** Wei Wang et al., "Parental Burnout and Job Burnout in Working Couples: An Actor–Partner Interdependence Model," *Journal of Family Psychology* 36, no. 5 (2022): 6–7, https://doi.org/10.1037/fam0000953.

95 **If we can find ways to:** Hawk Blog, "The Psychology of Simplicity: Why Less Is More in Work and Life," Hawk Safety, April 2, 2025, https://hawksafety.com/the-psychology-of-simplicity-why-less-is-more-in-work-and-life.

96 **"If you are too busy to":** Wanda E. Brunstetter, *Wanda E. Brunstetter's Amish Friends Cookbook: Desserts* (Barbour, 2011), 15.

96 **"The closer one approaches to God":** Sis. Juliet Jennifer, *The Prayers, Quotes and Sayings of Saint Teresa of Avila* (Sis. Juliet Jennifer, 2016) chap. 3, Kindle.

Day 18: Give Yourself Compassion

100 **When we criticize ourselves, we activate:** Logan J. Nealis et al., "Self-Critical Perfectionism, Depressive Symptoms, and HPA-Axis Dysregulation: Testing Emotional and Physiological Stress Reactivity," *Journal of Psychopathology and Behavioral Assessment* 42 (2020): 578, https://doi.org/10.1007/s10862-020-09793-9.

100 **Harsh self-scrutiny and worrying about how:** Ryan Tobin and David M. Dunkley, "Self-Critical Perfectionism and Lower Mindfulness and Self-

Compassion Predict Anxious and Depressive Symptoms Over Two Years," *Behaviour Research and Therapy* 136 (2021): 2, https://doi.org/10.1016/j.brat.2020.103780.

101 **When we're compassionate toward ourselves:** Emma Seppala, "The Scientific Benefits of Self-Compassion," Center for Compassion and Altruism Research and Education, Stanford Medicine, May 8, 2014, https://ccare.stanford.edu/uncategorized/the-scientific-benefits-of-self-compassion-infographic.

101 **Being self-compassionate helps us to respond less:** Larissa G. Duncan et al., "A Model of Mindful Parenting: Implications for Parent-Child Relationships and Prevention Research," *Clinical Child and Family Psychology Review* 12, no. 3 (2009): 260, https://doi.org/10.1007/s10567-009-0046-3.

101 **"Self-compassion is pretty straightforward":** Kristin Neff and Christopher Germer, *Mindful Self-Compassion for Burnout: Tools to Help You Heal and Recharge When You're Wrung Out by Stress* (Guilford, 2024), 15.

101 **Be kind to yourself:** Kristin Neff and Oliver Davidson, "Self-Compassion: Embracing Suffering with Kindness," in *Mindfulness in Positive Psychology: The Science of Meditation and Wellbeing,* ed. Itai Ivtzan and Tim Lomas (Routledge, 2016), 38–40.

Day 19: Replace Comparison with Confidence

106 **"the expectations of Western societies may":** Isabelle Roskam et al., "Three Reasons Why Parental Burnout Is More Prevalent in Individualistic Countries: A Mediation Study in 36 Countries," *Social Psychiatry and Psychiatric Epidemiology* 59 (2024): 687–89, https://doi.org/10.1007/s00127-023-02487-z.

106 **Evaluating ourselves based on what other:** Sarah M. Coyne et al., "'Do You Dare to Compare?' Associations Between Maternal Social Comparisons on Social Networking Sites and Parenting, Mental Health, and Romantic Relationship Outcomes," *Computers in Human Behavior* 70 (May 2017): 335, https://doi.org/10.1016/j.chb.2016.12.081.

107 **When we compare our parenting:** Jaime E. Sidani et al., "Associations Between Comparison on Social Media and Depressive Symptoms: A Study of

Young Parents," *Journal of Child and Family Studies* 29, no. 12 (2020): 3357, https://doi.org/10.1007/s10826-020-01805-2.

107 **"Every minute you spend comparing":** Heather Creekmore, *The Burden of Better: How a Comparison-Free Life Leads to Joy, Peace, and Rest* (Leafwood Publishers, 2020), chap. 1, Kindle.

Day 20: Embrace Your Flaws

110 **Apparently, this trick reverses certain hormones:** Robin S. Rosenberg, "Why You May Want to Stand Like a Superhero," Psychology Today, July 14, 2011, www.psychologytoday.com/us/blog/the-superheroes/201107/why-you-may-want-to-stand-like-a-superhero.

111 **When we accept our imperfections:** Emma Seppala, "The Scientific Benefits of Self-Compassion," Center for Compassion and Altruism Research and Education, Stanford Medicine, May 8, 2014, https://ccare.stanford.edu/uncategorized/the-scientific-benefits-of-self-compassion-infographic/.

Day 21: Trust Your Wonderful Counselor

118 **Yet the American Psychological Association reports:** "Stress in America 2023: A Nation Recovering from Collective Trauma," American Psychological Association, accessed November 11, 2025, www.apa.org/news/press/releases/stress/2023/collective-trauma-recovery.

119 **Sharing our personal problems with someone:** Zara Abrams, "The Science of Why Friendships Keep Us Healthy," American Psychological Association, *Monitor on Psychology* 54, no. 4 (2023): 42, www.apa.org/monitor/2023/06/cover-story-science-friendship.

119 **"It is simply not within human":** Dallas Willard, *Hearing God: Developing a Conversational Relationship with God* (InterVarsity, 1999), 43.

Day 22: Have a Good Cry

124 **Having a good cry and allowing:** Emily Nagoski and Amelia Nagoski, *Burnout: The Secret to Unlocking the Stress Cycle* (Ballantine Books, 2020), 18.

124 **In addition to lowering stress:** Lana Burgess, "Eight Benefits of Crying: Why

It's Good to Shed a Few Tears," Medical News Today, July 13, 2023, www.medicalnewstoday.com/articles/319631#benefits-of-crying.

Day 23: Find True Contentment

128 **Setting goals and pursuing aspirations:** Xavier Oriol et al., "Self-Transcendent Aspirations and Life Satisfaction: The Moderated Mediation Role of Gratitude Considering Conditional Effects of Affective and Cognitive Empathy," *Frontiers in Psychology* 11, no. 2105 (2020): 1–2, 9, https://pmc.ncbi.nlm.nih.gov/articles/PMC7477295/pdf/fpsyg-11-02105.pdf.

129 **People who regularly spend time growing:** Mariano Rojas and Karen Watkins-Fassler, "Religious Practice and Life Satisfaction: A Domains-of-Life Approach," *Journal of Happiness Studies* 23, no. 5 (2022): 2349, https://doi.org/10.1007/s10902-022-00510-9.

129 **"For Thou hast made us for":** Saint Augustine, *Confessions,* 2nd ed., ed. Michael P. Foley, trans. F. J. Sheed (Hackett, 2006), 3.

Day 24: Grow Your Joy

133 **"I come to the garden alone":** C. Austin Miles, "In the Garden" (Hall-Mack, 1912).

134 **Our moods lift, our anxiety lightens:** Timbers and Hollenberger, "Christian Mindfulness," 5.

134 **"Joy does not simply happen":** Henri J. M. Nouwen, *Here and Now: Living in the Spirit* (Crossroad, 1994), 31.

134 **"If we don't rejoice today":** John Ortberg, *The Life You've Always Wanted: Spiritual Disciplines for Ordinary People* (Zondervan, 2002), 69.

Day 25: Connect with Others

139 **In stressful parenting situations:** Avsar Ardic, "Relationship Between Parental Burnout Level and Perceived Social Support Levels of Parents of Children with Autism Spectrum Disorder," *International Journal of Educational Methodology* 6, no. 3 (2020): 538, https://doi.org/10.12973/ijem.6.3.533.

139 **"Spiritual togetherness, what I call *connecting*":** Larry Crabb, *The Safest Place on Earth: Where People Connect and Are Forever Changed* (Word, 1999), 22.

Day 26: Explore Your Emotions

146 **But when we deny our painful:** Brené Brown, *Braving the Wilderness: The Quest for True Belonging and the Courage to Stand Alone* (Random House, 2019), 67.

146 **Emotions are complex, and we experience:** Goran Šimić et al., "Understanding Emotions: Origins and Roles of the Amygdala," *Biomolecules* 11, no. 6 (2021): 823, https://doi.org/10.3390/biom11060823.

146 **This means experiencing our emotions:** Marsha M. Linehan, *DBT Skills Training Manual,* 2nd ed. (Guilford, 2015), 321.

147 **This simple practice of naming:** Linehan, *DBT Skills Training Manual,* 324.

147 **Putting feelings into words:** Matthew D. Lieberman et al., "Putting Feelings Into Words: Affect Labeling Disrupts Amygdala Activity in Response to Affective Stimuli," *Psychological Science* 18, no. 5 (2007): 421, https://doi.org/10.1111/j.1467-9280.2007.01916.x.

147 **"see painful emotions as compassionate invitations":** Alicia Michelle, *Emotional Confidence: 3 Simple Steps to Manage Emotions with Science and Scripture* (Baker Books, 2024), 37.

Day 27: Reframe Your Perspective

152 **"We need to be able to":** Joyce Meyer, *Power Thoughts: 12 Strategies to Win the Battle of the Mind* (FaithWords, 2010), 180.

152 **In Christian mindfulness, we learn to observe:** Regina Chow Trammel and John Trent, *A Counselor's Guide to Christian Mindfulness: Engaging the Mind, Body & Soul in Biblical Practices & Therapies* (Zondervan Reflective, 2021), 208.

153 **As we meditate on the new:** Trammel and Trent, *A Counselor's Guide to Christian Mindfulness,* 213.

Day 28: Cure Envy with Empathy

157 **It stems from a complex mix:** Robert L. Leahy, "Cognitive-Behavioral Therapy for Envy," *Cognitive Therapy and Research* 45 (2021): 418–19, https://doi.org/10.1007/s10608-020-10135-y.

158 **"The cure for envy lies in":** Charles H. Spurgeon, *Faith's Checkbook: Daily Devotional—Promises for Today,* updated ed., ed. P. Miller (Aneko, 2020), 135.

Day 29: Uncover Anger

162 **Exhaustion from parenting can easily lead:** Ana Júlia de Paula et al., "Parental Burnout: A Scoping Review," *Revista Brasileira Enfermagem* 75, suppl. 3 (2022): 2, https://doi.org/10.1590/0034-7167-2021-0203.

162 **Uncontrolled anger can cause any number:** "Anger Management: Strategies for Parents and Grandparents," Stanford Medicine Children's Health, accessed July 1, 2025, www.stanfordchildrens.org/en/topic/default?id=anger-management-strategies-for-parents-and-grandparents-160-45.

162 **This tension can also create distance:** De Paula et al., "Parental Burnout," 2, 8.

162 **Anger causes physiological changes:** Bahman Zohuri and Shiva Dalili, "Understanding Anger and Effective Anger Management Techniques (A Short Review)," *Management Studies* 11, no. 4 (2023): 242, www.researchgate.net/publication/373946371_Understanding_Anger_and_Effective_Anger_Management_Techniques_A_Short_Review.

163 **We can also experience cognitive effects:** Annrose Gregory, "Anger and the Brain, Body, and Decision: Neural and Physiological Effects," *International Journal of Commerce, Management, Leadership, and Law* 1, no. 1 (2024): 90, https://ijcmll.com/1/article/view/12/11.

163 **Breathing exercises help reverse the physical:** Zohuri and Dalili, "Understanding Anger," 242.

163 **But anger is typically a secondary:** Kyle Benson, "The Anger Iceberg," The Gottman Institute, last updated June 26, 2024, www.gottman.com/blog/the-anger-iceberg.

163 **"I sat with my anger long":** This quote is often attributed to C. S. Lewis but has not been confirmed in any of his writings. The author is actually unknown.

Day 30: Release Your Fears

168 **"when we focus on God":** Jackie Smith-Bell, "Inviting God's Peace Into Our Fear," Proverbs 31 Ministries, January 24, 2025, https://proverbs31.org/read/devotions/full-post/2025/01/24/inviting-gods-peace-into-our-fear.

Day 31: Welcome Freedom from Guilt

174 **Many parents wade through high levels:** Peter Stearns and Ruthann Clay, "American Guilt: A Challenge for Contemporary Emotions History," *Social and Education History* 6, no. 3 (2017): 316, https://doi.org/10.17583/hse.2017.2927.

174 **In contrast, guilt is unjustified when:** Marsha M. Linehan, *DBT Skills Training Manual*, 2nd ed. (Guilford, 2015), 371.

175 **To improve our psychological health:** Michelle Beer et al., "The Relationship Between Mindful Parenting and Distress in Parents of Children with an Autism Spectrum Disorder," *Mindfulness* 4 (January 2013): 110, https://doi.org/10.1007/s12671-012-0192-4.

175 **Simply put, extending ourselves forgiveness:** Denisa Marcinechová et al., "Self-Forgiveness, Guilt, Shame, and Parental Stress Among Parents of Children with Autism Spectrum Disorder," *Current Psychology* 43, no. 3 (2024): 13, https://doi.org/10.1007/s12144-023-04476-6.

175 **"Those who perceive God as compassionate":** Kristin J. Homan, "A Mediation Model Linking Attachment to God, Self-Compassion, and Mental Health," *Mental Health, Religion & Culture* 17, no. 10 (2014): 985, http://dx.doi.org/10.1080/13674676.2014.984163.

Day 32: Experience Indescribable Peace

179 **Eight in ten parents report they:** Zach Hrynowski, "Parents Avoid Hard—but Helpful—Conversations with Gen Z," Gallup, August 14, 2024, https://news.gallup.com/poll/645602/parents-avoid-hard-helpful-conversations-gen.aspx.

179 **Forty percent of U.S. parents:** Rachel Minkin and Juliana Menasce Horowitz, "Parenting in America Today: Mental Health Concerns Top the List of Worries for Parents," Pew Research Center, January 24, 2023, www.pewresearch.org/social-trends/2023/01/24/parenting-in-america-today.

179 **And the more we worry:** Brian Fisak et al., "What Do Parents Worry About? Examination of the Construct of Parent Worry and the Relation to Parent and

Child Anxiety," *Behavioural and Cognitive Psychotherapy* 40, no. 5 (2012): 542, https://doi.org/10.1017/S1352465812000410.

179 **I hope you've experienced how focusing:** Virginia Burgdorf et al., "The Effect of Mindfulness Interventions for Parents on Parenting Stress and Youth Psychological Outcomes: A Systematic Review and Meta-Analysis," *Frontiers in Psychology* 10, no. 1336 (2019): 19–20, https://doi.org/10.3389/fpsyg.2019.01336.

180 **"The secret is *Christ* in *me*":** Elisabeth Elliot, *Keep a Quiet Heart* (Revell, 1995), 20.

Day 33: Receive His Grace

185 **Living in the freedom of his:** Branwyn Hailee McCormick, "Direct and Mediating Relationships Between Divine Grace, Legalism, and Mental Health" (PhD diss., Liberty University, 2025), 35, https://digitalcommons.liberty.edu/honors/1500.

185 **Christians who better understand and appreciate:** Timothy A. Sisemore et al., "Grace and Christian Psychology-Part 1: Preliminary Measurement, Relationships, and Implications for Practice," *Edification: The Transdisciplinary Journal of Christian Psychology* 4, no. 2 (2011): 61–62.

185 **Embracing God's grace also strengthens our:** Adam S. Hodge et al., "Experiencing Grace: A Review of the Empirical Literature," *Journal of Positive Psychology* 17, no. 3 (2022): 11, https://doi.org/10.1080/17439760.2020.1858943.

Day 34: Renew Your Strength

189 **Fifty-seven percent of U.S. parents report:** Office of the Chief Wellness Officer and College of Nursing, "The Power of Positive Parenting: Evidence to Help Parents and Their Children Thrive," The Ohio State University, May 2024, https://nursing.osu.edu/sites/default/files/2024-05/OCWO_ParentalBurnout_3674200_Report_2024Update_FINAL_2.pdf.

189 **Parenting burnout can also lead to:** "Study: Pressure to Be 'Perfect' Causing Burnout for Parents, Mental Health Concerns for Their Children," The Ohio State University College of Nursing, May 8, 2024, https://nursing.osu.edu/news/2024/05/08/perfect-parent-study.

189 **Many of us have a hard:** Melissa Weekes, "The 'Me Do It' Mentality and Asking for Help," Great Kids, accessed July 17, 2025, www.greatkidsinc.org/the-me-do-it-mentality-and-asking-for-help.

190 **When others offer to help us:** Xuan Zhao, "Asking for Help Is Hard, but People Want to Help More Than We Realize, Stanford Scholar Says," Stanford University, Stanford Report, September 8, 2022, https://news.stanford.edu/stories/2022/09/asking-help-hard-people-want-help-realize.

190 **Relying on his presence throughout:** Thomas Frederick and Kristen M. White, "Mindfulness, Christian Devotion Meditation, Surrender, and Worry," *Mental Health, Religion & Culture* 18, no. 10 (2015): 856, http://dx.doi.org/10.1080/13674676.2015.1107892.

190 **"Relying on God has to begin":** Wayne Martindale and Jerry Root, eds., *The Quotable Lewis: An Encyclopedic Selection of Quotes from the Complete Published Works of C. S. Lewis* (Tyndale House, 1989), 156.

Day 35: Break Out of Darkness

194 **If you feel overwhelmed, you're in the company:** Office of the Surgeon General (OSG), "Parents Under Pressure: The U.S. Surgeon General's Advisory on the Mental Health & Well-Being of Parents," U.S. Department of Health and Human Services (2024): 9, www.ncbi.nlm.nih.gov/books/NBK606662.

194 **A higher percentage of mothers report:** Jamie R. Daw et al., "Trends and Disparities in Maternal Self-Reported Mental and Physical Health," *JAMA Internal Medicine,* 185, no. 7 (2025): 857, https://jamanetwork.com/journals/jamainternalmedicine/fullarticle/2834318.

194 **Maybe most concerning is that 40 percent:** Richard Weissbourd et al., "Caring for the Caregivers: The Critical Link Between Parent and Teen Mental Health," Harvard University Graduate School of Education, June 2023, https://mcc.gse.harvard.edu/reports/caring-for-the-caregivers.

194 **What's more, our mental health directly:** Office of the Surgeon General (OSG), "Parents Under Pressure," 8.

194 **With the daily stress you're under:** Gyeong-A Park and Oan Na Lee, "The Moderating Effect of Social Support on Parental Stress and Depression in

Mothers of Children with Disabilities," *Occupational Therapy International* (March 14, 2022): 2, https://doi.org/10.1155/2022/5162954.

194 **"Sweet friend, there is nothing wrong":** Sarah J. Robinson, *I Love Jesus, but I Want to Die* (WaterBrook, 2021), 11.

195 **Strengthening your mental health and faith:** Joshua B. Grubbs et al., "Self, Struggle, and Soul: Linking Personality, Self-Concept, and Religious/Spiritual Struggle," *Personality and Individual Differences* 101 (October 2016): 145, https://doi.org/10.1016/j.paid.2016.05.365.

Day 36: Laugh More

202 **Laughter reduces stress and improves mental:** "Healthy Lifestyle Stress Management: Stress Relief from Laughter? It's No Joke," Mayo Clinic, accessed July 16, 2025, www.mayoclinic.org/healthy-lifestyle/stress-management/in-depth/stress-relief/art-20044456.

202 **Following laughing, there's a decrease:** Mary Payne Bennett and Cecile Lengacher, "Humor and Laughter May Influence Health: III. Laughter and Health Outcomes," *Evidence-Based Complementary and Alternative Medicine* 5, no. 1 (2008): 37–39, https://doi.org/10.1093/ecam/nem041.

202 **Just a single session of laughter:** "Laugh It Up! 5 Benefits of Laughter for Older Adults," UCLA Health, February 21, 2025, www.uclahealth.org/news/article/laugh-it-up-5-benefits-laughter-older-adults.

202 **Approaching life and parenting:** Christine Yu, "Parents Who Use Humor Have Better Relationships with Their Children, Study Finds," Penn State, August 12, 2024, www.psu.edu/news/research/story/parents-who-use-humor-have-better-relationships-their-children-study-finds.

203 **"The most wasted of all days":** This quote is often attributed to the American poet E. E. Cummings but has not been confirmed in any of his writings. The author is actually unknown.

203 **Children laugh approximately four hundred times:** "Laugh It Up!," UCLA Health.

203 **"We don't laugh because we're happy":** This quote is attributed to William James and is a paraphrase from his 1950 book, *The Principles of Psychology,* and his 1948 journal article, "What Is an Emotion?"

203 **In other words, our brain takes cues:** Goran Šimić et al., "Understanding Emotions: Origins and Roles of the Amygdala," *Biomolecules* 11, no. 6 (2021): 3, https://doi.org/10.3390/biom11060823.

203 **Self-induced laughter can actually be even:** Ramon Mora-Ripoll, "Simulated Laughter Techniques for Therapeutic Use in Mental Health," *Journal of Psychology & Clinical Psychiatry* 8, no. 2 (2017): 2, https://doi.org/10.15406/jpcpy.2017.08.00479.

204 **"God brings laughter into our lives":** Janet Holm McHenry, *Looking Up!: Finding Joy as You Read and Pray Through the Bible* (Our Daily Bread, 2024), January 6.

Day 37: Plan Fun Activities

207 **Looking forward to an enjoyable outing:** Samuel S. Monfort et al., "The Impact of Anticipating Positive Events on Responses to Stress," *Journal of Experimental Social Psychology* 58 (May 2015): 21, https://doi.org/10.1016/j.jesp.2014.12.003.

207 **Imagining a fun activity releases dopamine:** Jennice Vilhauer, "Finding Joy: How Positive Anticipation Boosts Your Happiness," Psychology Today, updated October 25, 2024, www.psychologytoday.com/us/blog/living-forward/202405/finding-joy-how-positive-anticipation-boosts-your-happiness.

208 **"Should we not play in beautiful":** Kevin Gushiken, *A Theology of Play: Learning to Enjoy Life as God Intended* (Kregel Academic, 2024), chap. 1, Kindle.

Day 38: Move in Gratitude

212 **Expressing thanks increases our positive emotions:** Jeffrey Klibert et al., "The Impact of an Integrated Gratitude Intervention on Positive Affect and Coping Resources," *International Journal of Applied Positive Psychology* 3, no. 1 (2019): 34–36, https://doi.org/10.1007/s41042-019-00015-6.

212 **Showing appreciation to others also strengthens:** Joyce L. T. Leong et al., "Is Gratitude Always Beneficial to Interpersonal Relationships? The Interplay of Grateful Disposition, Grateful Mood, and Grateful Expression Among Married Couples," *Personality and Social Psychology Bulletin* 46, no. 1 (2020): 65, https://pubmed.ncbi.nlm.nih.gov/31046594/.

212 **Specifically, regularly journaling prayers of thanksgiving:** Sarah A. Schnitker and Kelsy L. Richardson, "Framing Gratitude Journaling as Prayer Amplifies Its Hedonic and Eudaimonic Well-Being, but Not Health, Benefits," *Journal of Positive Psychology* 14, no. 4 (2019): 427–28, https://doi.org/10.1080/17439760.2018.1460690.

213 **"Gratitude is the gateway to joy":** Lisa Appelo, *Life Can Be Good Again: Putting Your World Back Together After It All Falls Apart* (Bethany House, 2022), 115.

Day 39: Discover Beauty

217 **When we remain fully awake:** Rosalie Weigand and Thomas Jacobsen, "Beauty Lies in the Eye of the Mindful: Does Mindfulness Intensify Aesthetic Experience by Freeing Working Memory Resources?," *Psychology of Aesthetics, Creativity, and the Arts* 19, no. 6 (2023): 1539–48, https://doi.org/10.1037/aca0000639.

217 **Practicing mindfulness and deep breathing opens:** Aleksandra Igdalova et al., "*Room to Breathe:* Testing the Efficacy of Mindful Breathing and Mindful Design in Enhancing Museum Experiences," *Journal of Positive Psychology* 20, no. 6 (2025): 2, 11, https://doi.org/10.1080/17439760.2025.2502489.

217 **"God is the object of our beauty":** Steve DeWitt, *Eyes Wide Open: Enjoying God in Everything* (Credo House, 2012), 18.

Day 40: Treasure Simple Moments

222 **When we live in the present:** Marc Wittmann and Stefan Schmidt, "Mindfulness Meditation and the Experience of Time," in *Meditation—Neuroscientific Approaches and Philosophical Implications,* ed. Stefan Schmidt and Harald Walach, Studies in Neuroscience, Consciousness and Spirituality 2 (Springer International, 2013), 201, 206, https://doi.org/10.1007/978-3-319-01634-4_11.

223 **"If only I have eyes to":** Tama Fortner, *Everyday Joys* (Ink & Willow, 2024), 29.

About the Author

KRISTIN FAITH EVANS, MA, MS, LMSW, is an award-winning author, national speaker, licensed master social worker, and a busy mom of two. She empowers parents with the skills to thrive in their faith, mental health, and marriages. She graduated with honors with her master's in Christian Ministry and Spiritual Formation from Wheaton College and her master's in social work from the University of Tennessee. Kristin and her husband co-wrote their multi award-winning book, *How to Build a Thriving Marriage as You Care for Children with Disabilities.*

Kristin has appeared on over forty different radio and podcast shows including *Focus on the Family, Family Life Radio,* and *Moody Radio.* She has been featured in numerous publications including *Exceptional Needs Today, Christian Counseling Connection,* and *Focus on the Family.* Her professional experiences have included child and family, couples, substance abuse, and crisis interventions as well as church and retreat ministries. She enjoys a cup (or two) of Italian roast, dark chocolate, traveling, and authentic conversations with friends. She lives in the suburbs of Nashville, Tennessee, with her fun-loving husband of twenty-five years and their two children.

Connect with Kristin and find lots of free resources at
DisabilityParenting.com.